IRISH GHOSTS

John J. Dunne

IRISH GHOSTS
John J. Dunne

For the very latest on Irish Ghosts visit our Ghostwatch webcam at:
www.irelandseye.com/ghost/index.shtm

APPLETREE

To the memory of my father
and the day he gave me **Treasure Island**

First published in 1977
Appletree
The Old Potato Station
14 Howard Street South
Belfast BT7 1AP
Tel: (0) 28 90 243074
Fax: (0) 28 90 246756
Web Site: www.appletree.ie
E-mail: reception@appletree.ie

A catalogue record for this book is
available from the British Library.

Irish Ghosts

ISBN 0-86281-766-8

10 9 8 7 6 5 4 3 2 1

Contents

PUBLISHER'S NOTE

This new edition of *Irish Ghosts* includes a peculiar ghost story which even staff in Appletree Press will vouchsafe as true. When we decided to publish the new edition, a few of us discussed the haunted linen mill which is near our own offices in Belfast. The mill was once home to a thriving linen industry but today a printing company is based there. We have used this printing company for several years and through friendship and business, we learned about the ghost in the mill. The witnesses to the ghost in the linen mill are astute men and women who would usually disbelieve in ghost stories but their own inexplicable encounters are told calmly and without hysteria. The printers suggested that we spend some time in the linen mill and experience the haunting.

A rigorous investigation indicated that Helena Cecilia Blunden, a young woman had died in the mill in 1912. The eldest daughter of a Tyrone woman and a Kilkenny man, Helena had been born in Ireland but brought up in England. In 1911, the Blundens returned to Ireland and settled in Belfast. They moved into a small terraced house in Raphael Street which was only a few hundred yards from the linen mill.

We resorted to technology to observe the ghost and installed a camera in a room in the mill which is used infrequently. A few employees from the printing company and Appletree Press spent some time watching the camera during daylight but no one was prepared to spend time in the building at night. We found a solution in setting the camera up on our internet site and inviting visitors to ghostwatch. The camera allowed us to ghostwatch 24 hours a day, seven days a week. This live broadcast by the internet was first set up at Hallowe'en. The web camera ran and ran. Thousands of visitors contacted us with reports of sightings which truly astonished us. They often reported the fleeting appearance of a young woman in the spinning room, logging time and date of sightings. They described her clothes, hairstyle and shoes, which are more suited to an Edwardian woman than the fashion worn by a woman at the end of the twentieth century. The woman has often been seen in the building when staff have all gone home. The web camera continues to run and web site visitors still report sightings. Of course, there are many visitors who reported seeing nothing unusual on the web camera but many people have seen things which defy obvious explanation.

When you have read the account of Helena Blunden's life and death, you too may want to ghostwatch by viewing the web camera. Join the Ghostwatch at www.irelandseye.com and contact us with your report of what you have seen.

Catherine McIlvenna
Editor

Acknowledgements

I wish to acknowledge the help and courtesy I have received from the following in the preparation of this book:

The officials and staffs of the National Library of Ireland; the Central Catholic Library; the City of Dublin Public Libraries (Raheny and Pearse Street branches); St Patrick's College, Maynooth, Co. Kildare; Clongowes Wood College, Sallins, Co. Kildare.

My thanks are due to Sean Ward, Editor of the *Evening Press*, Dublin, for permission to use excerpts from reports; to William Connolly, Managing Director of the Talbot Press, for allowing me to use an excerpt from *Heavy Hangs the Golden Grain* by Seamus MacManus; to Matt Farrell and Sean McCann of the *Evening Press* for their assistance and encouragement; to John Murphy and William Derra of the Appletree Press, Belfast, for their painstaking attention to the manuscript; and to David Marcus of the *Irish Press*, whose idea sparked it off in the first place.

I am grateful, too, to the many people who introduced me to some of the ghosts that appear in these pages.

And my special thanks are due, indeed, to Lawrence O'Connor, who so generously placed at my disposal his remarkable collection of period photographs.

Introduction

The banshee and the headless coach, phantom dogs and fear-some black cats, shadowy figures flitting along the dim corridors of old houses, gentle ladies that glide at midnight down gracious staircases, strange death warnings, unaccountable sounds in the dark in the secret recesses of storied castles. . . such are the ghosts of Ireland, an integral part of her tradition and her atmosphere.

Of them all, the banshee (in Gaelic, *bean-sidhe*, or fairy woman) is undoubtedly the most characteristically Irish. Generally depicted as being a small, wizened old woman, slowly combing her long hair and uttering the most doleful cries, she was widely accepted as being a certain harbinger of death, if not to those who heard her, then to some close relative or neighbour.

For comment on the banshee, we can go back over a century to Hall's *Ireland* in 1840:

> The banshee is the wildest and grandest of all the Irish superstitions. The spirit assumes the form of a woman; she is usually attired in loose, white drapery, and her duty upon earth is to warn the family upon which she attends of the approaching death of one of its members.
>
> This warning is given by a peculiarly mournful wail. . . at night. It is a sound that resembles the sough of the wind, but having the tone of the human voice, and distinctly audible at a great distance.
>
> She is sometimes seen as well as heard, but only by a person of the 'old stock'. . . the representative of some ancient race: and him or her she never abandons, even in poverty

The banshee, the phantom coach, the headless horseman, the lady in white, all were the stock in trade of the old Irish story-teller.

or degradation. Thus MacCarthys, the O'Sullivans, the O'Riordans, the O'Learys, and other septs in Munster have each their banshee.

Although the 'popularity' of the banshee has diminished greatly in recent years, up to a few decades ago the older people in the country districts, and even in the cities among those whose parents had come from rural areas, still retained an unshaken belief in the old superstition.

In Dublin, in the late 1920s, the persistent reports of the appearance of a banshee in the suburban village of Coolock, received extensive coverage in the newspapers.

Indeed, many Irish families with the tradition of having a banshee attached to them were proud of the fact, as she was accepted as a testimonial of their true Irish lineage and stock, and accounts of her appearance, especially if followed by a death in the family, were recorded with pride and gusto.

There are, of course, other traditional Irish death warnings, such as the three unexplained taps on a door at night, or the mysterious falling of a picture from its place on a wall. In a land rich in superstition, these are merely one facet of Ireland's treasure-house of the folklore of the supernatural.

In a countryside richly sprinkled by stately old mansions, many of them with long and often bloody histories, the preva-lence of the ghost story is not surprising. Many of these houses, perhaps because of their isolation and their frequently decayed condition, have their own particular ghost stories, told and retold around the firesides of the district.

Even Dublin city, and especially Georgian Dublin, is rich in these legends, and ghost stories exist about such buildings as Iveagh House on St Stephen's Green (now the Department of Foreign Affairs), the Shelbourne Hotel, the public library in Kevin Street, the Olympia Theatre, Marsh's Library and many others.

The tall Georgian houses of such city squares as Mountjoy Square, Merrion Square and Fitzwilliam Square, some of them dating from the beginning of the last century and earlier, occa-sionally turn up a story of the supernatural. One such account was contained in *Real Ghost Stories* by Major MacGregor:

Towards the end of 1871 I went over to Ireland to visit a

relative living in a square in the north side of Dublin. In January 1872, the husband of my relative fell ill. I sat up with him for several nights, and, at last, as he seemed better, I went to bed, and directed the footman to call me if anything went wrong.

I soon fell asleep and sometime afterward was awakened by a push on the left shoulder. I started up and said, 'Is there anything wrong?' I got no answer, but immediately received another push. I got annoyed and said: 'Can you speak, man, and tell me if there is anything wrong?' Still no answer, and I had a feeling I was going to get another push when I suddenly turned around and caught a human hand, warm, plump and soft. I said, 'Who are you?' but got no answer. I tried to pull the person towards me, but could not do so.

I then said: 'I will know who you are,' and having the hand tight in my right hand, with my left I felt the wrist and arm, enclosed, as it seemed to me, in a tight-fitting sleeve of some winter material, with a linen cuff; but when I got to the elbow, all trace of an arm ceased. I was so astonished that I let the hand go, and just then the clock struck two.

When I reported the adventure, the servants exclaimed: 'Oh, it must have been the master's old Aunt Betty; she lived for many years in the upper part of the house and died over fifty years ago at a great age.'

I afterwards learned that the room in which I felt the hand had been considered haunted and very curious noises and peculiar incidents occurred, such as the bedclothes being torn off, etc. One lady got a slap in the face from an invisible hand.

The locale of that story was, without doubt, Mountjoy Square, the only truly impressive square to the north of the Liffey. Built sporadically at the close of the eighteenth century and the beginning of the nineteenth, it soon fell from favour, and the once gracious houses became, for the most part, tenements. By the late 1960s, two sides of the square, the south and west sides, had been largely demolished, although on the remaining sides several had been restored to some reminder of their Georgian glory by Dublin Corporation, the Jesuit Fathers, a city wine merchant and others. One house, on the west side, was happily purchased by the Hon. Desmond Guinness, who was responsible for the preservation of several fine mansions, notably that of Castletown, in Celbridge, Co. Kildare.

Adjoining Mountjoy Square is Summerhill, once also a fashionable residential street, where lived the famous coachbuilding family of Huttons, and, indeed, a group of houses owned by the family forms the locale of one of the recordings of supernatural visitations included in this volume.

Dublin's finest 'square', St Stephen's Green, has several strange stories of its own.

One of these centres on a room in the internationally famous Shelbourne Hotel, about which an account has been published concerning the ghost of a little girl, supposedly a resident of the original house before it and its immediate neighbours were converted to form the Shelbourne.

The foregoing are merely random examples of the countless ghost stories to be found all around Ireland, in the tall old houses of Dublin's history-soaked streets, in the rambling, grandiose mansions half lost in ancient walled demesnes that survive still in their hundreds throughout the countryside, in all sorts of odd corners here and there in a land particularly rich in folklore and where passion and emotion have throbbed strongly, strongly enough, few will question, to leave their vibrations.

The Summerhill Ghost

That ghosts still walk today, and do not belong exclusively to the past, is illustrated by the extraordinary story of the apparitions at Summerhill, a street in north Dublin. Here there were several down-to-earth witnesses of the manifestation, able to testify to what they had seen to the daily newspapers.

In January 1966, a demolition firm was called in to demolish No. 118 Summerhill, an old, tall Georgian tenement house, originally one of a row of three. Nos. 116 and 117 had already been knocked down. Within a few days the demolition work came to an abrupt halt, as terrified workmen reported having seen the apparition of a man wearing a striped apron, similar to those once popular with butchers.

One of the workmen, Mr Joseph Byrne, told the *Evening Press*:

I was wrestling with an old stove in the basement when I had a feeling someone was standing behind me. I looked around and saw nothing. After a while the same feeling crept over me and I had another look around. I saw a man, dressed in what appeared to be a butcher's striped jacket, standing looking towards a window. I shouted to the others, who were all working above me, but when they came down they couldn't see it at all.

Two of Mr Byrne's fellow workers, however, did see the apparition on separate occasions, and their descriptions tallied. One of them, Mr William McGregor, fainted from the shock.

The three old houses, of which No. 118 was one, had a long and even romantic history, and one of them had the local reputation of being haunted, though, strangely, this was No. 117 and not the house where the ghostly 'butcher' was seen.

The houses had been tenements for years, having been converted into flats when they were acquired in 1923 by the Dublin United Tramways Company, from which time they had been known locally as 'the tramway houses'.

For many years before that, however, they had been owned by the famous Hutton family, proprietors of the coach-building firm whose reputation was widespread for the superb coaches it turned out at its adjoining workshops. One Hutton-built coach is still used on state occasions by the British royal family.

Thomas Hutton, the head of the firm, lived in one of the houses, and there, in the 1840s, Thomas Davis, the Young Ireland leader, came to court Annie Hutton, one of Thomas Hutton's daughters.

Afterwards, it was No. 117 that became known as the haunted house. It was customary for passers-by to quicken their pace when they had to pass it at night, and occasionally crowds gathered on the opposite footpath on the off chance of 'seeing the ghost'. It is an interesting fact that No. 117 had been already demolished when the apparitions of 1966 were reported in No. 118.

The third Hutton house, No. 116, had also been knocked

down by then, but it too had strange stories told about it.

Patrick Cullen, author of the Gate Theatre success *The Dalers*, told me that the play, which sought to expose the evils and injustices of moneylending in Dublin, was, in fact, based on No. 116 Summerhill, where the author had lived for some years as caretaker when it had been turned into flats.

'The house had a bad reputation for ghosts,' Mr Cullen said, 'especially the basement, which was certainly considered to be haunted.'

The caretakers's flat was on the top floor, and people going upstairs to it were aware of strange sensations when they reached the landing underneath, and of a decided drop in temperature, similar to the famous 'cold spot' on the landing at Borley Rectory.

Mr Cullen tells of one eerie experience of his own in No. 116. He and his wife were entertaining a couple of relatives in the living room, when he had occasion to leave the room and cross the landing to another apartment. When he had been in this room alone for several minutes, he was startled when he heard three raps on the door beside him. These were repeated with slow deliberation.

Thinking that one of his guests was playing a joke, he hurried from the room, only to find that nobody had left the living room since he himself had done so. No one, other than the member of the family in the living room, had any access to the flat at the time.

One ghost or several? Did the ghostly occupant of the 'haunted' house pass into the house next door when No. 117 was demolished? What strange events took place in the tramway houses during the long winter nights of the nineteenth century to leave their imprint in these once-gracious old Georgian rooms. . . to leave restless spirits lurking in the shadows?

It is a fact of history that a man named Patrick Conway cut his throat in No. 118 Summerhill in 1863. He was a butcher.

The Black Dog of Cabra

Cabra today, is a thickly populated suburb on the north side of Dublin, with trim, well-kept homes, its own shops and pubs. It even had its own cinema until the 1970s when this closed and became a bingo hall. Its western end adjoins the wall of Phoenix Park, and the main road northwards to Navan and Kells passes through it.

Until the late 1920s Cabra was a semi-rural fringe of the city, incorporating the townland of Beggsboro. In the 1930s building began, and a large Corporaton scheme brought many new residents to the area. It was towards the close of the decade that this expansion precipitated the demolition of an old Cabra house, one with a grim history that, in its time, had been shunned by people living close to it.

The story has died with the development of the area as a suburb, and is probably unknown now to most occupiers of the trim, two-storey houses that today stand on the site, but it is mentioned in Patrick Byrne's *Irish Ghost Stories*, and may still be remembered by older Dubliners with a special interest in the folklore of the district.

A phantom black dog was said to roam the leafy lanes surrounding the house and was an unending source of terror to local residents in the nineteenth century. But, although they feared it, those who avoided travelling the lonely roads at night whenever possible, in case they would meet it, thought they knew its identity. The dog, they claimed, was the ghost of the one-time owner of the old house, and this was none other than the notorious Lord Norbury, the infamous 'Hanging Judge'.

Thus it came about that John Toler, first Earl of Norbury, became as much feared after his death as he had been in his lifetime by the unfortunates who stood before him in the dock. Norbury survives in history chiefly because it was he who tried Robert Emmet and others involved in the 1798 rebellion.

Off the bench, when he was at home in Cabra, Norbury was intensely disliked by his neighbours, especially if they happened to come into close contact with him. But the odium in which he was held spread much further afield, for his reputation as a merciless and ruthless judge was such as to strike terror into those hapless victims of his 'justice'. According to R. Dudley Edwards, author of *Daniel O'Connell and his World*, another biographer of O'Connell, unnamed, dubbed Norbury 'the Irish Judge Jeffreys'.

So the hatred of Norbury lived on long after his death, and the shadowy lanes around his home in Cabra were for many decades permeated with his presence, especially in winter, when local people crossed themselves in the still hours of the night and listened with tensed nerves for the awe-inspiring sound, the slow pat-pat of the paws of a large black dog.

THE PHANTOM CITY

A story I heard on the cliffs of the west,
    That oft, through the breakers dividing,
A city is seen on the ocean's wide breast
    In turretted majesty riding.
But brief is the glimpse of that phantom so bright,
    Soon close the white water to screen it
And the bodement, they say, of the wonderful sight,
    Is death to the eyes that have seen it.

I said, when they told me the wonderful tale,
    My country, is this not thy story?
Thus oft, through the breakers of discord, we hail
    A promise of peace and of glory.
Soon gulphed in those waters of hatred again,
    No longer our fancy can find it,
And woe to our hearts for the vision so vain;
    For ruin and death come behind it.

                                        Gerald Griffin

Strange Knockings in Fishamble Street

The ghost of Hamlet's father is not the only one associated with the stage, and many old theatres have stories of the supernatural associated with them. Indeed, the unreal world of the theatre, and the highly emotional make-up of actors themselves, perhaps contribute to the frequent instances of paranormal experiences recounted, on both sides of the footlights.

Perhaps the most famous ghost is that which is said to have attached itself to London's Theatre Royal in Drury Lane, where the figure of a man has been seen frequently, by a wide assortment of people, and over a lengthy span of years. This apparition always appears in daylight, and follows the same route, from one side of the auditorium to the other, although, on occasion, it has been seen sitting in a seat. Strangely enough, the appearance of this Drury Lane ghost is taken to foretell that the current show will be a success. Some years ago, the skeleton of a man was found, with a dagger in the ribs, in a long blocked up part of the old building and this grisly discovery may indeed provide a pointer to the apparition.

The phantom walker in the upper circle is not, however, the only ghost attached to Drury Lane. During the last century, an actor was murdered in the Green Room, beside a fireplace, and the room is said to be haunted to this day. There have been reports, too, of the appearance in the theatre of the ghost of the comedian Dan Leno.

Another London theatre to have a ghost attached to it is the Haymarket, where an apparition resembling the famous nineteenth century actor-manager John Baldwin Buckstone has been seen frequently in a dressing room he always used.

It is inevitable, too, that a city with the strong theatrical tradition of Dublin should have its share of theatre ghosts, and while accounts have appeared of strange noises and unexplained footsteps being heard by actors working in the old Olympia, once Dan Lowry's famous Empire, and well known down its many years by performers ranging from Jessie Mathews to G. H. Elliott, Dublin's most famous ghost story belongs to an even older theatre, the long demolished house of entertainment in Fishamble Street.

The Fishamble Street Theatre was situated close to the ancient Fyans Castle, later Proudfoote's Castle, and was opened in 1741 as Mr Neale's Music Hall. In April of 1742 it was the setting for an event for which it is still remembered, the first performance of Handel's *Messiah*, a charity performance in aid of Mercer's Hospital, the Charitable Infirmary and prison relief.

Other great nights came to Fishamble Street. One of these was the 28 February 1812, when Daniel O'Connell came to address a packed theatre. By his side sat a young Englishman, caught up in the magnetism of the Irish cause, and fresh from distributing a pamphlet he had written about Ireland to the passers-by in Sackville Street. His name was Percy Bysshe Shelley.

Supernatural manifestations at the Fishamble Street Theatre go back almost to the start of the last century, and appear to have been centred on its Green Room, which had seen so many great theatrical personalities in its time. Here, inexplicable knockings on the walls were frequently heard, always beginning at ten o'clock in the evening and continuing for fifteen minutes.

One who had experienced the phenomenon in the old theatre was a builder's apprentice named John Hogan, who was frightened by the knockings while working there during alterations in the middle of the last century, and who passed the story down through his family.

Fishamble Street today is half demolished, but this time-worn thoroughfare that slopes down to the Liffey, in the very shadow of Christ Church in the heart of the Liberties, must still hold ghosts for many. . . the sonorous voice of a 37-year-old O'Connell, the presence of a young English poet espousing Ireland's cause, and Handel's *Messiah* spreading out to all the world.

Curse of the Whip

The story of the weird revenge taken by one sister on another, embracing frustrated love and smouldering hatred, a jewelled riding-whip from Russia, a curse and a macabre deception, is centred around a remote spot in Co. Tipperary, where a proud mansion once stood.

The house, at Ballymacorthy, near the village of Clogheen, close to the famous Vee pass, was called Shallardstown and was built in the early 1800s by Cadogan Parrott, who went to live in it when he married a local girl named Angelica Gammage. The couple had two daughters, the elder named

Angelica, after her mother, and the younger called Rosaleen.

Sorrow, however, soon came to Shallardstown, when Mrs Parrott committed suicide, followed shortly after by her husband, leaving Angelica mistress of the fine house.

Casting an eye around for a suitable husband, Angelica fell in love with a local man named Dagan Ferritter, but her romantic plans went sadly astray when Ferritter became captivated by her younger sister, and subsequently married her in 1837.

On the small allowance made to them by Angelica, the young couple travelled to the Continent, where they decided to stay for a while. The following year Angelica herself went to London.

It was during this stay in London that Angelica Parrott met a young diplomat and fell in love with him. He was a Russian, Prince Nicholas Orloff, and an attaché at his country's embassy. They were soon married, and the prince and his bride spent a brief honeymoon in St Petersburg. They presently returned to Paris, but had not been there long before Prince Orloff caught a chill and died.

Angelica Parrott travelled back to Ireland and, on arrival at Shallardstown, dismissed whatever servants were there, with the exception of a butler, a man named Creed. She herself never left the house and never received visitors. Creed did the shopping in nearby Clogheen.

Meanwhile, her sister Rosaleen and her husband returned to Ballymacorthy, but Angelica, or, as she could now call herself, Princess Orloff, refused to see them. They lived in a small hut, barely existing on the miserable allowance which they received from Shallardstown, but patiently awaiting the day when Angelica's death might bring Rosaleen the ownership of the family home.

It was about this time that Princess Orloff began taking a drive in her landau. The vehicle emerged from the gates of Shallardstown each day at precisely three o'clock in the afternoon with the butler Creed acting as coachman and Angelica seated behind him. Always, she held in her gloved hand a richly jewelled riding-whip, which she had brought home from Russia as a sentimental reminder of her brief honeymoon in St Petersburg. The landau would drive through the surrounding countryside and return to Shallardstown at four o'clock, precisely.

This strange routine went on for many years, with Princess Orloff never deviating from her daily custom, and the poverty-stricken condition of her sister Rosaleen and her husband, the man who had spurned Angelica, becoming progressively worse.

A startling climax was reached, however, when one day some local men began to ridicule Dagan Ferritter for not having the courage to confront the remote mistress of Shallardstown and demand his wife's rightful inheritance. Goaded into action, and accompanied by some of his friends, Rosaleen's husband went to the big house and demanded to see the princess.

Under pressure, Creed told an amazing story. Angelica had been dead for eleven years, but, following her strict instructions, he himself had, every day, placed her corpse in the landau, with the jewelled riding-whip in her hand, and driven around the district for exactly one hour. This bizarre story was confirmed by a letter left by the princess, which Creed was able to produce, testimony to a well-thought-out revenge on Rosaleen and Dagan, a scorned woman's determined effort to cheat them of Shallardstown long after her own death.

The letter contained instructions that her jewelled whip should be placed in a showcase in the hall at Shallardstown with a curse on anyone who touched it.

Rosaleen and Dagan moved into the big house, but they were fated not to enjoy its comfort for long. Within a year both were dead. The whip of Orloff was placed in the hall, just as its owner had wished.

Shallardstown passed into the hands of a cousin and later, in 1896, was purchased by a religious order, and became a novitiate. In the years that followed strange stories began to be whispered about the house. There were several accounts of a shapeless figure being seen in the hallway, standing in front of the showcase containing the Orloff riding-whip, and the sounds of a departing carriage being heard on the driveway outside.

The mansion subsequently became vacant, and a caretaker claimed to have seen a ghostly figure on the stairs on at least two occasions, and to have frequently found the lid of the showcase in the hall open, especially around four o'clock in the afternoon.

A Georgian Haunting

Many of the tall, gracious, red-brick houses of Georgian Dublin have been the settings for ghosts and hauntings, but what must surely lay claim to being among the most haunted of all Dublin houses is one which was eventually demolished in 1963. It, together with several adjoining houses, saw several regularly recurring supernatural manifestations over a lengthy span of years, according to a tenant who lived in it for almost half a century.

Hendrick Street, until extensive demolition in the early 1960s, was a typical Dublin northside street, lined by old Georgian houses that had once been the homes of prosperous merchants and professional men, but which, by the outbreak of the First World War, had been turned into flats.

In 1914, a family named Brophy moved into a flat in No. 7 Hendrick Street, like its neighbours, even then, an old house. As far back as 1845, it had been occupied by a Mr Watt. They were not in occupation very long before they realised that it was the scene of peculiar happenings that could not easily be explained on rational grounds.

The most frequently recurring phenomenon occurred after dark, when suddenly the silence of the sleeping house would be broken by the eerie sound of bare feet, beginning always at the top of the house and coming rapidly down the stairs to the main hall.

The sound would fade away, but would be heard again after an interval of about fifteen minutes, when once more the scurrying feet would sweep down through the house. They were never heard going upstairs.

This manifestation continued from the early 1920s until the 1950s, and was heard by everybody in the house, the sound sometimes originating in an upstairs flat which was unoccupied and locked at the time.

A son of the Brophy family, Mr George Brophy, lived in No. 7 from 1914 until the house was condemned as a dangerous building by Dublin Corporation and demolished in 1963. He told me of one nerve-shattering experience he had with the phantom footsteps, probably the closest encounter anybody had ever had with them.

A photograph from the early years of the present century of traditional 'Cursing Stones' in south Co. Dublin. A person wishing to curse an enemy knelt before these and called for misfortune to befall his victim, sometimes wishing the evil to pass on to succeeding generations.

The Phoenix Monument, on the main road to Phoenix Park, Dublin, beside the Vice-regal Lodge, now Aras an Uachtarain, pictured in the Victorian high noon of empire, when a Viceroy ruled from a mansion now occupied by the President of Ireland. . .and haunted by the memory of murder at the spot close by where, in 1882, the Chief Secretary, Lord Frederick Cavendish, and the Under Secretary, Edward Burke, were knifed to death by members of the secret society known as 'The Invincibles'.

One night, in the early 1940s, having cycled to another part of the city to spend the evening with friends, Mr Brophy returned to No. 7 at about 1.30 a.m. Dismounting from his bicycle at the front steps, he hoisted the machine on to his shoulders, as was his custom, and carried it up the stairs to his flat.

He was on the point of inserting his key when, to his horror, he suddenly heard the dreaded sound of the bare footsteps somewhere in the darkness at the top of the house, just as he had heard them so many times before.

Knowing the footsteps would now descend the stairs very rapidly and pass across the landing where he stood, he tried desperately to turn his key in the lock and gain the safety of his flat.

Despite his feverish efforts, however, he was unable to open the door in time, and perspiration broke out on his forehead as the sound of the footsteps began to come swiftly down the stairs towards him.

Almost at once they reached the landing, and what Mr Brophy described to me as 'a gush of cold air' whipped across the landing behind him, as the footsteps died away towards the hall below.

Mr Brophy was, in fact, more courageous than most occupants of the house, who would not venture out of their flats after dark if they could avoid doing so. The phenomenon of the footsteps was heard regularly for years.

Mr Brophy was also witness to a poltergeist manifestation in No. 7.

One night, in 1932, he was sitting up late in the candlelit living room of the family flat. He was alone, and at about 12.50 a.m., decided to prepare some food for himself before going to bed. With this in mind, he crossed the room towards the dresser, and while he was still several feet away from it, a steel-handled knife, that had been placed on top of the press section of the dresser, was suddenly flung four or five feet into the air above his head, and then clattered back to its original position on the top of the dresser press.

In the early 1920s, a woman who acted as caretaker of the house and of No. 8 next door, died, and several times in the months that followed residents both saw and heard her working in the back yards at night.

Nor did the hauntings at No. 7 Hendrick Street end there. When an old lady who lived in the attic died, she was subsequently seen, on numerous occasions over a span of years, slowly ascending the stairs at night.

The adjoining house, No. 8, was credited with another haunting. One of the flats in it was occupied for several years by a man and his wife who were not always on the best of terms with each other, and there were frequent rows. The husband died suddenly, and for many years afterwards his wife was troubled in the flat, claiming that she frequently saw her husband in the living room, sometimes standing in a corner, at other times sitting by the fire.

Eventually, unable to stand the strain any longer, the woman called in a local priest. After that, she was never again troubled.

The final recorded manifestation at No. 7 Hendrick Street occurred in June 1963, just before the house was demolished, when, Mr Brophy told me, he saw a figure, 'like a cloud that grew gradually larger and then vanished', in the hallway.

It is an interesting footnote to history that, close to No. 7 Hendrick Street, in the back parlour of No. 11, lived a Mrs Ellis, a sister of the young bricklayer named Joe Brady from North Anne Street, who was executed for the murder of the Irish Chief Secretary, Lord Frederick Cavendish, and the Under-Secretary, Mr Edward Burke, in Phoenix Park in 1882. Mrs Ellis died at an advanced age in the 1950s.

As the Dublin Corporation bulldozers moved in to level these once stately Georgian homes, what other ghosts did they disturb as long-crumbling red-brick walls showered finally into dust and debris.

The Foxes of Gormanston

Luke Wadding College, Gormanston, Co. Meath, run by the Franciscan Fathers, is one of the most modern scholastic establishments in Ireland today, with a high reputation for adjusting itself rapidly to the ever-changing demands of modern education and also for the excellent facilities available to its students.

As one approaches the college, one can see that its main building is a stately, turreted castle. This is, in fact, Gormanston Castle, an early nineteenth century structure built on the site of a fourteenth century manor house that had been the home of the Preston family, the Viscounts Gormanston, since 1363, and whose occupancy of the castle lasted until it was sold to the Franciscan Order in the late 1940s.

The first Preston to come to Ireland was Roger de Preston, who moved house from Preston, in Lancashire, in 1326 and settled in Co. Meath, where he subsequently built the original manor house. A later Preston was created the first Viscount Gormanston by Edward IV in 1478, for devoted service to the House of York.

The story concerning the family is that scores of foxes come out of their coverts and gather around the castle whenever the death of a Viscount Gormanston is imminent. Here they remain, whining continuously, until after the Viscount's death, when they return to their coverts.

Perhaps the most eerie feature of this well-substantiated legend is that these are no 'ghost' foxes but live, flesh-and-blood animals, obeying some strange, inexplicable summons to gather at the castle door and hold a bizarre vigil whenever death is near for the head of the family. The legend maintains that they first appeared at the death of a Gormanston who had once saved the life of a vixen in a hunt.

The appearance of the foxes dates from the seventeenth century, and their presence has survived in many records, including those of the Preston family. It also merited mention in an historical survey of the castle published in the Franciscan College Annual shortly after the castle had been acquired by the Order in the late 1940s and in which acknowledgements are made to the writings of the late Father Paul Walsh and to an essay by Father Aubrey Gwynn, S.J., published in *Studies* in 1942.

In her book, *Strange Stories of the Chase*, the Countess of Feversham, sister of the Earl of Halifax , author of the famous *Ghost Book*, includes an account of the Gormanston foxes, given to her by Eileen, Viscountess Gormanston, wife of the 15th Viscount.

Whatever the explanation of the foxes of Gormanston, their

weird appearances have been vouched for time and time again, and the animal is incorporated in the coat-of-arms of the Preston family.

The story is unique in Irish tales of the supernatural, in which death warnings usually concern tappings on doors and walls, pictures falling from their places, apparitions of the person about to die, the so-called headless coach and, of course, the banshee.

The Beresford Story

In Marlborough Street, opposite Dublin's Pro-Cathedral, stands the Department of Education, part of which was Tyrone House. Here, for many years, when the mansion was in private ownership, hung a portrait of Lady Beresford, the former Nicola Hamilton. In it, a black ribbon encircled her wrist.

This ribbon was the source of one of the most celebrated of Irish ghost stories, a relic, it was claimed, of a pact between Lady Beresford and Lord Tyrone that whichever of them should die first would return from the grave and provide evidence of a life after death.

Lord Tyrone was the first to die, and, true to their bargain, appeared to Lady Beresford in her bedroom at Gill Hall in Co. Down. Apparently to assure her that she was not imagining the apparition, or dreaming, Tyrone touched her on the wrist, and then vanished.

Lady Beresford subsequently discovered, to her horror, that the sinews of that part of her wrist which had been touched by the ghostly fingers had withered, and, if she had ever doubted the nocturnal visitation, she now had enduring evidence of its reality. With understandable feminine concern, Lady Beresford, in order to conceal the grisly memento of her experience, wore a black ribbon tied tightly around the mark for the rest of her life.

Recounting the Beresford story in his *Ghost Book*, Sir Shane Leslie quotes from the manuscript diary of Mr J. L. Burges, Parkanaur, Co. Tyrone, for 16 July 1863:

We drove to Gill Hall, the residence of the Magills, now of Lord Clanwilliam. The house was built in the time of William III. There is a good Hall and dining room and old-fashioned staircase and a gallery room on the first landing. In a bed-chamber off this apartment the ghost of Lord Tyrone appeared to Lady Beresford and a small cabinet is shewn with a mark upon it, but it is not the real one which it is said was removed by Lady Clanwilliam's grandmother years ago.

While there is no record of the famous picture of Lady Beresford wearing the black ribbon having survived, Sir Shane Leslie claimed that he had seen the ribbon itself, preserved as a family heirloom.

It is perhaps an interesting sidelight on the apparition at Gill Hall that a Beresford became Marquis of Waterford, associated with one of the best-known Irish curses. This is said to have been placed on the family by the mother of a man hanged by a Beresford in Seskin, near Carrick-on-Suir, for some minor offence. It warned that the Beresford heirs would die violent deaths, and this, indeed, has been fulfilled by several tragedies suffered by the family in later years.

Who Was Grey Tullough?

From the folklore of Co. Kilkenny comes the strange story of a grey-haired old man who appeared from nowhere, was known to nobody, stayed for a time and then vanished just as abruptly and as mysteriously as he had arrived.

The district was a remote one, its most distinguished features being the ruins of an old church, a graveyard and an ancient tower, and throughout the time he spent there, the stranger did nothing but tidy the churchyard, cutting down the weeds, thistles and high grass which, until his coming, had overrun the lichen-covered tombstones.

The stranger, who had no friends, kept very much to himself and became known as Jimmy Tullough, although some called him Grey Tullough. At first, the local people paid little attention to him, putting him down as being simply another travelling man, but gradually they came to realise that there was something special, and perhaps a little frightening, about him. The first indication of this was when they noticed how their children respected him, never daring to make him the butt of their pranks, as, with the thoughtlessness of childhood, they were fond of doing with other simple travelling men who passed through the village.

A contemporary description of Grey Tullough from Hall's *Ireland* tells us that, encountered on the roadway, he passed by quietly, 'more like a shadow than a man. . . his hair hanging about his long, lean face; his ould reaping hood hung across his shoulder, and a straight shillalee like a spear in his hand; on he'd go, turning neither to the right nor the left, keeping his eyes settled on the path before him. If you said "God save ye kindly" to him out of good-nature, he'd make no answer either by word or sign, but keep on. . . on. . . on. . . walking, as if to eternity.'

Grey Tullough would take no money from anyone and, when offered it by the good-hearted local people, would say: 'Copper pays friends. . . silver makes friends. . . gold breaks friends.' But the occasions when he spoke to anyone were few.

Just before he vanished, the old man spent the entire night cutting down the weeds in the graveyard with his ancient reaping hook. Next morning, taking pity on him for having passed the hours of darkness in the eerie surroundings of the churchyard, and especially as it was midsummer's eve, an elderly couple who lived close by brought Grey Tullough into their cottage.

Seating himself slowly, he stared straight ahead, as though looking at something in the far distance. He spoke no word until the man of the house remarked to his wife that perhaps the old man had seen something during the night in the graveyard. Then Tullough said: 'I never see anything worse than myself.'

Presently, giving a great sigh, and without eating a bite of the food offered to him, the old man rose to his feet and left the little cottage, making his way into the churchyard and standing in the shadow of the old tower.

Some little time later, puzzled by this behaviour and thinking she might coax him to take a little food, the woman went outside to call him back. To the amazement of both her husband and herself, there was no sign of him anywhere.

The strange old man was never seen again in the little Co. Kilkenny village, and thereafter grass and weeds grew unchecked around the sombre, weather-beaten tombstones, and the gloomy tower forever retained the secret of Grey Tullough.

OH, YE DEAD!

Oh, ye dead! oh, ye dead! whom we know by the light you
    give
From your cold gleaming eyes, though you move like men
    who live,
  Why leave you thus your graves,
  In far-off fields and waves,
Where the worm and the sea-bird only know your bed,
  To haunt this spot, where all
  Those eyes that wept your fall,
And the hearts that bewailed you like your own, lie dead!

It is true – it is true – we are shadows cold and wan;
It is true – it is true – all the friends we loved are gone.
  But, oh! thus even in death,
  So sweet is still the breath
Of the fields and the flowers in our youth we wandered o'er,
  That, ere condemned we go
  To freeze mid Hecla's snow,
We would taste it awhile, and dream we live once more!

Thomas Moore

Ghost of Marsh's Library

Close to Patrick Street Corner, where the legendary Biddy Mulligan plied her trade 'for forty-five years' on the famous Dublin street called The Coombe, the spire of St Patrick's Cathedral towers high above the two plates in the flag-stones that mark the supposed resting place of Jonathan Swift and his beloved Stella. And just around the corner stands the eighteenth century building that houses Marsh's Library, one of the first free public libraries in Europe.

It is a place of ghosts, the ghosts of the Dean and Stella, of Michael Moran the ballad singer who became Zozimus and who died in lodgings in Patrick Street, of Quakers and Huguenots who built strange houses here, of saints and drunkards and money-lenders and street-traders and slum-dwellers who existed ten-to-a-room in the festering homes of the Liberties.

But Marsh's Library has a particular ghost of its own, the ghost of an old man who has been seen at midnight browsing through its ancient bookshelves, the ghost of its founder, Archbishop Narcissus Marsh.

Marsh was Archbishop of Dublin from 1694 until his appointment to Armagh nine years later, but the transfer did not terminate his interest in Dublin and in 1707 he founded his library, on ground belonging to the House of St Sepulchre, then the Palace of the Archbishops of Dublin.

The occasion is recalled in a transcript: 'An Act passed 1707 for settling and preserving a Publick Library for ever, in the House for that purpose built by His Grace Narcissus now Lord Archbishop of Armagh, on part of the Ground belonging to the Archbishop of Dublin's Pallace, near to the City of Dublin.'

For a hundred years after its opening Marsh's Library was the only free library in Dublin, and in 1739 Walter Harris, in his edition of Ware, said of it: 'I am under the necessity of acknowledging from long experience that this is the only useful library in the kingdom, being open to all strangers and at all reasonable times'.

It is perhaps not surprising that Narcissus Marsh should return after his death to a place apparently so close to his heart in life, or that the spectral figure seen sometimes searching through the old volumes in the inner gallery of the library has been identified as his.

A popular explanation of the archbishop's ghostly appearance concerns a favourite niece of his, a girl whom he had reared from a child. When the girl fell in love with a sea captain, the archbishop strongly disapproved and tried to prevent her from seeing the man. The young couple then made up their minds to elope and the girl, doubtless to assuage her conscience,

The interior of Marsh's Library (c. 1888) founded in 1707 in the grounds of St Sepulchre by Archbishop Narcissus Marsh – 'a Publick Library for ever' – and the first of its kind. Still in use today, it is an invaluable archive for the scholar, to which the Archbishop sometimes returns in dusky twilights, forever seeking a lost letter from a beloved niece.

wrote a note to her uncle, pleading for his forgiveness, and placed it in one of his books in the library.

Archbishop Marsh, however, never found the note that might have consoled him for the loss of his beloved niece, and the popular theory to account for his spectral presence in the old rooms he once knew so well is that he returns in death in an endless search for it.

The Phantom Piper

The sound of ghostly pipes heard in a cave on moonlit nights is a Co. Donegal story, told of what has become known as the Piper's Cave, one of a series of caves called the 'Pullans', through which the Blackwater River flows in the Brownhall demesne, beside the village of Ballintra.

It is an historic and picturesque district, and contains, besides the Pullans caves, McGonigle's Fort, said to be the burial place of Hugh Mac Ainmire, a sixth century high king of Ireland, and the mound of earth called Racoo, where St Patrick founded a monastery.

The story is that the sound of the ghostly pipes in the cave are those of a piper who once ventured inside the underground chambers and was never seen again.

In *My Times and Other Times*, John S. Hamilton remembered his father, speaking of the local tradition, saying that 'the piper went in and never came out and you hear him playing on moonlit nights'.

Recalling the more recent history of the cave, he recorded: 'In 1927, there was a big storm that blew down a big beech within fifty yards of this cave, lower along the river. As it grew on the rocks, the roots couldn't go down but were massed in a wonderful network, and the root stood up ten feet or more.'

Mr Hamilton recalled, too, that in 1929 a party of botanists, looking for specimans in the haunted cave, sent up word to him that they had discovered the skeleton of a man under the tree. When he descended to the spot, he saw the skeleton right across the very centre of the root, presumably the skeleton of the piper. Later, he had the bones examined, and was told that they were between 400 and 600 hundred years old.

The ghostly piper of Ballintra belonged to the rich musical heritage of Ireland, like Tom Carthy, born near Ballybunion, Co. Kerry, who, for 65 years, was a familiar figure as he played on Castle Green, Ballybunion. He lived in three centuries, being born in 1799 and dying in 1904, at the age of 105. (Photo: Kevin Garvey)

Hell Fire Club on the summit of Mount Pellier, Co. Dublin, built as a hunting lodge by the speaker Connolly and a favourite rendezvous for roistering eighteenth century evenings with the young bloods of Dublin.

What long-ago reason brought a piper into the lonely cave at Ballintra, and what unknown fate overtook him while he was inside, claiming his life and leaving his bones hidden for centuries, the sound of his music wafting through the mysterious shadows of moonlit nights.

The Black Cat of Killakee

For centuries, one of the most dramatic and unchanging landmarks of south County Dublin has been the gaunt ruin of the notorious Hell Fire Club that broods grimly on the slopes of Mount Pellier in the Dublin Mountains.

The Hell Fire Club has a black history, though perhaps painted blacker by legend than it deserves. It is part of Dublin lore that the old building was a rendezvous for the members of an exclusive club, founded in 1735 by the 'bucks' and 'young bloods' of Dublin City, for their endless gambling, roistering and merrymaking.

Weird stories survive of their nocturnal activities, embracing orgies and strange rites, the appearance of the Devil, and phantom coaches rocking wildly through the night. At least one of these stories records murder, when a servant was set on fire by club members. Another records the appearance of a demon in the guise of a cat, and, indeed, it is a phantom black cat that figures most prominently in eerie tales of the area.

In fact, the members of the Hell Fire Club usually met at the Eagle Tavern on Cork Hill, although it is certainly likely that visits were organised to the lonely building on Mount Pelier.

The isolated house on the mountain top that was to become known as the Hell Fire Club was built by William Connolly, Speaker of the Irish House of Commons, as a hunting lodge, and indeed, several other reminders of his fondness for building survive, most notably Castletown House in Co. Kildare, which, as described in another chapter, has its own legend of demoniac visitation.

On the slopes beneath Connolly's hunting lodge, stories of a ghostly black cat abound and the ferocious creature has been encountered on lonely laneways, on the adjoining estate of Lord Massey and in other old buildings in the district. Here, in the townland of Killakee, stood the old Massey mansion which eventually fell into ruin, and it is in this immediate vicinity that the legend of the phantom cat persists, perhaps inspired to some extent by the fact that a cat was included in the stone carvings incorporated into the house.

Part of the Massey dower house was in recent years converted into an art centre yet, despite this modern usage, stories of strange occurrences persist.

On 29 April 1970, Dublin newspapers reported that the owner of the Killakee Art Centre, Mrs Margaret O'Brien, who had just spent two nights alone there, while her husband, Nicholas, a retired Garda Superintendent, was in Cork visiting his mother, had been terrified by noises each night, and had found considerable damage done in padlocked rooms which showed no evidence of a break-in.

Furniture was broken, crockery smashed and other items were damaged, and Mrs O'Brien, visibly shaken, according to a reporter who interviewed her, told the *Evening Press*: 'I have had a terrible night. There has been a lot of damage done. I am going back to bed, as I have hardly slept at all. I don't even want to talk about it. If I leave now, I'll never go back. I'll stick it out.'

She said that she had been awakened by a 'crashing sound and dogs howling' in the middle of the night. The coffee bar and the stone hall were wrecked. The floors were littered with broken crockery, chairs were smashed, and an electric fire damaged, while paintings were scattered all over the room. It looked as if somebody had run amok in the rooms. In the lounge bar, bottles of spirits were smashed. In fact, the only bottle not destroyed was one containing holy water. The howling of the dogs, which had awakened her, sounded 'as if they were scared out of their skins'.

Another strange feature of Mrs O'Brien's ordeal was that two cats, which she had fed and put in the kitchen the previous evening, turned up mysteriously in a tower that stands beside the 200-year-old house. The doors of the tower were locked.

'How the cats managed to get out of the house is a mystery to me and even a bigger mystery is how they came to be locked in the tower,' said Mrs O'Brien.

The O'Briens, according to the newspaper reports, had uncanny experiences from the very beginning of their occupancy of Killakee. When they moved into the 15-roomed house in 1968 and began to make alterations, workmen refused to stay there, because of 'ghostly' happenings. When three friends of the family came to stay, they saw a three-foot tall crippled man standing at the door of the stone hall and they claimed that he then turned into a cat. This experience led to the exorcising of the ghost from the house, and peace was restored and remained until, early in 1970, a group of friends held a seance in the house. This was followed by the continuous flashing of lights, the ringing of bells and other unnerving noises.

Mrs O'Brien herself claimed that she had seen two nuns and a handsome Indian walking through the building. They turned slightly towards her, she said, and then disappeared 'into thin air'.

On the day following publication of this report, the *Evening Press* carried another story suggesting that the disturbances at Killakee had been provoked by the visit of a Radio Telefís Éireann crew, filming a feature for the programme *Newsbeat*, and accompanied by Sheila St Claire.

The nocturnal manifestations followed the filming of Mrs St Claire 'in communication' with spirits in the building. During the session she had performed automatic writing, and messages about the house and its history were transmitted. When she was in a semi-trance, the messages concerned the apparitions that had been seen there over the years, like that of nuns sprinkling holy water on the old tower.

An Austrian priest, Father Settelle, who had experience of such occurrences in Germany, and who was visiting Ireland at the time, told Mrs O'Brien that he thought Mrs St Claire had been in tune with the 'poltergeist entity' in the house, which, he said, upset the spirits, so that the noises and extensive damage followed. He warned her not to allow outsiders to stay in the house, and to let things quieten down.

'When the entity is on the same wave-length as the medium, they can do this kind of thing.' Mrs O'Brien told a reporter on 30 April 1970. 'Father Settelle told me that when the medium went away the occurrences would stop.'

A brass effigy of the devil, which was clasped to a painting of a huge black cat in the stone hall, was found in a holy water font in another room. Mrs O'Brien was told by Mrs St Claire to take down a brass figure of a cat from the door of the galleries. It had been taken from a head-stone over the grave of a crippled boy who had lived in the house 150 years ago. Occasionally, the apparition of a boy has been seen at the old dower house.

Mount Pellier and Killakee are lonely places, expecially at night, just such a location, indeed, that might easily conjure up the rumbling of Lord Santry's coach on its way to the Hell Fire Club. . . or the fancied glint of two phantom feline eyes in the darkness.

The Fairy Sheep

The ghostly voice of a man calling in vain for a lost sheep is an old legend of the Mitchelstown Caves, at Coolagarranroe, near Ballyporeen, in the shadow of the Galtee mountains in Co. Tipperary.

There are two groups of caves at Mitchelstown, the old or Desmond group and the new group. The new caves were discovered on 2 May 1833 by a man quarrying for stones, and the French speleologist Martel drew a sketch plan of them in 1895.

However, the ghostly legend of the sheep belongs to the old cave, sometimes called the Desmond cave, after the 'Sugan Earl' of Desmond who took refuge there in 1601 when there was a price on his head. It centres around the discovery of the cave, situated on part of the estate of the Earl of Kingston.

A poor man who lived close by, and who depended for his livelihood on his 'quarter of potatoes' (the quarter-acre attached to his home) was wandering through the fields one day when he was surprised to hear the bleat of a sheep, at a spot where there was no grazing. Following the sound, he presently found its source, a large hole, at the bottom of which lay a sheep with a broken leg.

Jumping into the hole, the man attempted to lift the animal, and at once was struck by the amazing softness and whiteness of her wool. As he lifted her out of the hole and laid her on the grass, she never once cried, but looked up at him with large, beautiful eyes.

To avoid being seen, the man kept clear of the only road in the district, the one leading to the Earl of Kingston's castle, as he carried the injured sheep home.

His wife thought at first that he had stolen the animal, but when he explained the strange way in which he had got it, she decided that they would tend to the stricken creature, and vehemently protested her husband's intention of killing it. Like her husband, the woman had noticed the extraordinarily fine quality of the wool, and told him she would take a handful or two of it to make stockings.

Under the woman's tender care, the sheep got better, and nobody ever came forward to claim it. The gentle animal would stand perfectly still for shearing, and the woman industriously made stockings from the wool. The wool was so good that the fame of the stockings quickly spread throughout the countryside, and the demand for them became so great that very soon the woman and her husband had more money than they had ever had before.

In time, the sheep produced lambs, and these, too, had wool of such splendid texture and colour that it earned far more for the couple than the meat would have done. For years the man and his wife prospered.

Inevitably, the original sheep grew old, and her once lovely wool became thin and shaggy. The man decided to kill her, and, despite the heart-broken entreaties of his wife, vowed that he would do so the very next day.

The following morning, however, the couple were awakened very early by the boy they employed to tend the sheep. The lad ran to their house in a great state of excitement, and told them that the entire flock, despite his efforts, had moved off, led by the old sheep herself.

The man instantly hurried out and, accompanied by the boy, set off in the direction taken by the sheep. When they had crossed several fields they caught sight of the flock, but even as they looked, the animals disappeared one by one as though swallowed up by the ground.

When they reached the spot, the last sheep had vanished.

The boy watched as his employer passed through a crevice in some rocks, in a desperate effort to overtake the animals. When he did not emerge after several minutes, the boy hastened away to summon the help of neighbours. When a party of local men returned with the lad to the place soon afterwards, there was no sign of either the sheep or their owner. They followed the crevice in the rocks where he had last been seen, and it was then that they discovered the entrance to the cave.

Fetching candles from a nearby house, the group entered the cave and, in the distance, heard the voice of the man calling out to the sheep. Despite an extensive search, however, they failed to find him and neither he nor the sheep were ever seen again.

Over the years that followed this first discovery of the old cave at Mitchelstown, it was believed locally that the ghostly voice of the man calling to his sheep in the vast dark chambers beneath the earth was heard on occasion by people venturing near the entrance after dark. It was claimed too, that the sheep was not an earthly animal, but a fairy creature, a belief encouraged by the animal's gentle disposition and the extraordinary quality of its wool.

MITCHELSTOWN CAVERNS

Grimly it frown'd when first with shuddering mind
   We saw the far-famed Cavern's darkling womb,
   And for that vault of silence and of gloom
Left the fair day and smiling world behind.

But what bright wonder hail'd our eyes erelong!
   The chrystal well – the sparry curtained dome –
   The sparkling shafts that propp'd that cavern'd home,
And vaults that turn'd the homeliest sounds to song.

Oh, this, I thought, is sure a symbol plain
   Of that undreaded death the holy die,
   Stern at the first and withering to the view;
But past that gate of darkness and of pain,
   What scenes of unimagined rapture lie –
   Rich with elysian wealth and splendour ever new.

Gerald Griffin

A Glaslough Ghost

One of the most distinguished collectors of ghost stories was the late Sir Shane Leslie, of Glaslough, Co. Monaghan, who maintained a life-long interest in supernatural manifestations of every type and after long involvement with the subject published his findings in his well-known *Ghost Book*.

Glaslough House, a stately mansion set in a magnificent timbered demesne in the village of Glaslough, seven miles from Monaghan town and close to the Armagh-Tyrone border, is the home of the Leslie family and is the setting of a ghostly encounter experienced by the ghost-hunter himself.

It is a unique manifestation in as far as the ghost seemed to be well informed on current happenings, according to Sir Shane's own account of the occurrence, which he included in his delightful autobiography *The Film of Memory*.

More accustomed to writing about apparitions seen by other people, he tells us about what happened to himself one night in the family home at Glaslough:

Curiously enough, Uncle Moreton, who died in 1925, was one of the few of the dead whose apparition I have seen.

There is a type of apparition which is visible to a sleeper in the first moments succeeding sleep. It has nothing to do with the previous dreaming nor has it any particular reason for appearance.

It has occurred to me three times, and each time so vividly as to be overwhelming. For several hours after each appearance I could not collect myself sufficiently to continue with ordinary life. My sense told me I had seen figures from the other world. This has only occurred to me after waking and while feeling perfectly assured that I was awake.

I awoke at Glaslough two years after Uncle Moreton's death, and to my surprise I saw him standing in the room. I was completely in possession of my senses and could see every object.

Uncle Moreton said very deliberately to me: 'I don't mind what you have written about me, but Uncle Stee will mind very much!'

I had recently written a sketch of his career which I had

classed under 'Sublime Failures'. This message was apparently correct, for Colonel Stephen Frewen, Lord Carson's father-in-law, was much annoyed, which I learned later.

It was all so vivid that I could not think of anything else for several hours.

As readers of his *Ghost Book* will know, Sir Shane's research in the realms of the supernatural was done with a detached and almost clinical approach, and his interest ranged over the whole gamut of manifestations, from apparitions and death warnings to poltergeists. This record of something he experienced himself is, therefore, all the more impressive.

The Tragic Bride of Charles Fort

She walks the ancient ramparts of Charles Fort and may be seen sometimes in the half-light of dusk, a tragic figure in white, doomed forever to glide silently through the place where she found brief love terminated by shattering tragedy.

Charles Fort stands about a mile and a half outside the town of Kinsale, in Co. Cork, at Summer Cove, and is an old garrison that was used as a barracks up to the time of the withdrawal of British troops from Ireland.

It is, perhaps, not surprising to find a ghost in Kinsale, for this haunted town on the estuary of the River Bandon is rich in history and tradition, with a charter going back to Edward III. Its narrow streets must hold silent memories of its heyday, before the construction of larger ships rendered its docks inadequate.

Once, in 1601, Spanish ships sailed into Kinsale, and held the town against the strength of England's Carew and Mountjoy, but despite the arrival of the armies of the earls of Tyrone and Tirconnell, the Spanish were eventually forced to surrender. A one-time Clerk of the Admiralty Court of Kinsale, one William Penn, was to become the founder of Pennsylvania; his father, Admiral Penn, was Governor of Kinsale.

And from the human drama of all those years of Kinsale's past, emerges the sad legend of the lady in white of Charles Fort.

The girl's father was Commander of the Fort, and the privileged life of his daughter in the pleasant town on the Bandon was uneventful, until the day she met a handsome young officer who had come on a visit to Kinsale. It was romance from the start. They fell in love and were married.

On their wedding night, the happy couple walked, arm in arm, on the ramparts of Charles Fort, aglow with love and having the promise of a long life ahead of them.

As they reached the landside wall of the fort, the young bride suddenly stopped in ecstasy, pointing over the rampart to where a solitary white rose grew on a bush below the high walls.

A sentry, on duty close beside them, overheard the girl expressing a wish for the rose and immediately volunteered to climb down and get it for her, if her husband would stand in as sentry for him while he was doing so.

The bridegroom agreed to this and took the man's musket. The sentry clambered over the wall and disappeared. Standing at the sentry-post, with his bride beside him, the young husband awaited the man's return, while his bride looked forward eagerly to soon having the coveted rose placed in her hands.

Time passed, but the sentry did not return. Presently, assuming the man had met with some unforeseen delay in securing the rose, the bridegroom sent the bride indoors to their quarters, deciding to wait a while longer himself at the sentry-post.

Leaning on the sentry's musket, the young husband, after a while, dozed off, and a short time later when the girl's father, as Commander of the Fort, came on his tour of inspection, he found him asleep. Without realising that the nodding man was not the sentry, but his own son-in-law, and in dutiful execution of the severe military code of the day he shot the sleeping man.

A moment too late the commander saw that it was not the sentry he had killed, but the young officer whom his daughter had married only that very day. Demented by his discovery, the commander threw himself off the ramparts.

Some time later, the bride, who had emerged from her quarters in search of her husband, found his body on the ramparts and, a little while later, that of her father on the rocks beneath the walls. Idyllic happiness had turned to stark tragedy. The grief-stricken bride, too, jumped to her death.

And on the grey ramparts of Kinsale's historic Charles Fort,

Charles Fort, at Summer Cove, near Kinsale, Co. Cork, where echoes of an old tragedy survive in accounts of the ghost of a girl in white who endlessly walks its ruined battlements. (Photo: Bord Failte)

Poulaphouca Waterfall, Co. Wicklow, where the Liffey tumbles in a series of picturesque cataracts, is a popular beauty spot. Its name is derived from Ireland's fairy lore, the Pool of the Pooka, or Fairy House. Pictured towards the close of the last century.

her graceful wraith still walks, they say, a pathetic ghost in a grim place of tragedy.

The Black Dog of Pussy's Leap

The district of Templeogue has for long been an extensive suburb of south Dublin, but before the expansion of the city it was a quiet, old-world village of small houses and shops in the foothills of the mountains, and, in common with most rural areas, had its own local stock of legends and traditions.

In Templeogue, these were many, and several of them centred around the nearby spot known as Pussy's Leap. In the late 1930s they formed the subject of long correspondence in the letters-to-the-editor pages of the old *Dublin Evening Mail*. One of the stories of Pussy's Leap that emerged – ironically it featured a black dog – was told by a reader who signed off as 'Black Cat'.

As an old resident and one who spent my childhood in the district, I would like to relate an experience of 40 years ago at Pussy's Leap.

At that time there was only one delivery of letters in the morning, and if you required the night letters you had to call to the post office in Templeogue.

It was a moonlit winter evening about 9 p.m., and I was walking home with the letters, accompanied by a servant maid from Cherryfield. As my companion and I approached Pussy's Leap, a black dog crossed our path. It got larger as it ran across, and gradually went out of sight, with the sound of chains.

I need not state here my fears, but I managed to get home without losing consciousness. For years after, I was always afraid to pass the 'leap' at night. Strange, the servant maid did not see the dog, but heard the rattling chains.

Another old legend relates that some 70 years ago a man was killed by a runaway horse at Pussy's Leap, where the Knocklyon road intersects, and I remember well, as a boy, seeing a rough cross in the grass border. The old residents and people of Firhouse, Old Bawn and Piperstown, used to drop a stone on the cross as they passed. The advent of steam-rolled roads, minus loose stones, prevented the keeping up of this old custom.

A good many of your readers may not be aware that right under the road at Pussy's Leap runs a small stream from the lands of Ballyroan and Charleville to the corner of the lands of Cherryfield. In summer time one can walk under the road. The Dodder side of this stream used to be overhung with blackberry briars, and on many occasions in the company of boyhood companions we used to shout and catcall through the arch when dusk was falling, and I think we frightened many a windy angler wielding his cast at nightfall.

The location of this 'black dog' ghost story at Pussy's Leap is not far from those of the black cat of Killakee and the headless coach of Tallaght, recounted in other chapters.

The Lady of Killyleagh

Who is the gracious lady who glides silently across the old hall of Killyleagh Castle, on the historic shores of Strangford Lough? Locally, it is thought that she is the ghost of Anne, the first Countess of Clanbrassil who defended her home in a courageous and remarkable defiance of Cromwell.

The original castle at Killyleagh was built by John De Courcy, the Anglo-Norman leader, although it was substantially rebuilt in 1850, when two of its original towers were retained. Yet, the changes apparently did not succeed in banishing the ghost of the woman who had once loved it.

As part of his stand against Cromwell, on behalf of Charles I, Anne's husband, Clanbrassil, attempted the relief of Carrickfergus, but was put to flight. When the news reached his wife at Killyleagh she immediately called together all the villagers and brought them into the castle, turning it into a stronghold. The siege that followed is an enduring tribute to a remarkable and valiant woman. Despite the concentrated onslaught of the Parliamentary Army, and even against such redoubtable leadership as that of General Monck, the countess's makeshift garrison held out. Nor was there ever a surrender by the brave band of villagers in the castle, inspired by the determination of the woman who led them. The stalemate was only ended by a truce called for by the countess.

The charm as well as the strength of this first Countess of Clanbrassil is shown by the fact that she was able to persuade Cromwell not only to reduce by half the fine of £10,000 which had been levied against her, but also to grant pardon to her husband.

The lough that the ancient building overlooks also has a troubled past. Although the Irish themselves had called it Loch Cuan, the harbour lake, the Norsemen renamed it Strang Fiord, the violent inlet.

And perhaps on dark winter nights, when the waters of the 'violent inlet' below are sullen and restless, Anne's ghost plays with the shadows in the old building she defended so bravely. Perhaps then she is joined by other ghosts, from other days in Killyleagh's past.

The castle was the birthplace, in 1666, of Sir Hans Sloane, afterwards a famous London physician who, during world-wide travels, accumulated a vast collection of books, manuscripts and coins that formed the nucleus of the British Museum.

In more recent times, the historic building on the lough became the home of the distinguished Rowan-Hamilton family. Whoever its occupants, one of the most intriguing features of the old home must be the ghostly figure in the hallway.

The Blue Lady of Ards

In consorting with the ghosts of Ireland, we come across white ladies and grey ladies but from the beautiful Ards peninsula, that juts out into Sheephaven Bay, near Creeslough, in Co. Donegal, comes the unique mystery of the blue lady.

It was in this magnificent setting, in the shadow of Muckish Mountain, that the Stewart family wisely chose to build their house, on lands given to them for services rendered to the crown. Indeed, the house and lands became one of the showplaces of Donegal, but the days of the great landlords spun out, and eventually the 'big house' of the Stewarts passed into the hands of the Capuchin Order.

Probably it was from the time of the Stewarts that our ghost comes, how or why no one knows, although she did not make her presence felt until after the mansion had been taken over by the Capuchins and had become their house of theological studies for Irish novices.

Stories about the ghostly lady, according to local residents, have a ring of truth. One of them suggested to me that perhaps this is because priests are involved.

It is reported that the apparition was seen on top of the oak staircase in the mansion. The stairs were horseshoe-shaped, that is two flights, one on either side, formed a horseshoe meeting at the landing above.

A priest is said to have seen the ghost, a lovely lady in blue, at the top of the stairs, just as he was about to ascend them. In order to avoid her he crossed over to the other flight. However, she then appeared again at the top of the stairs in front of him. He crossed over to where he had been originally, but once more she confronted him. He then decided to pass by her, and did so.

Every night, the blue lady could be heard walking gently down the hall and was frequently seen passing into, or out of, one of the rooms. Eventually the friars decided that something should be done about the apparition, although apparently they did not want her banished.

Details from this point are somewhat vague, but it seems that some ceremony must have been conducted, for afterwards the blue lady made no further appearances.

An intriguing aspect of the affair, however, is the fact that in the house a room was sealed and its window and door blocked up.

Up to 1966, when the new chapel and monastery was built, replacing the old mansion that had been the home of the Stewarts, people could frequently be seen gazing up at the blocked-up window and discussing the apparition. Visitors speculated on the identity of the ghost, and why she appeared, but the mystery was never solved. And, of course, the friars would never say anything about the appearances, parrying questions about their ghost from curious visitors. They merely smiled.

The old house is gone now; and so, too, is the mysterious blue lady of Ards.

The Ghostly Mass

Throughout the length and breadth of Ireland, one comes across tales of the supernatural in which the Mass figures prominently, and, not surprisingly, many of these have close associations with Penal times. Strange music is heard from a locked church at night, a priest sees the ghost of his predecessor on the altar, and old houses have legends of a 'hidden room', the 'priest's room', in which a hunted priest sought refuge when pursued by soldiers.

One of the best of these has been recorded by Seamus Mac-Manus in his *Heavy Hangs the Golden Grain*.

MacManus was a superb historian of his own Donegal countryside, and the folktales he garnered proved a rich literary harvest. His story of a ghostly encounter at a Mass rock in Co. Donegal provides an example, too, of his storytelling art at its best.

I heard of a Gweebarra man who was travelling over the mountains on the night of All Souls' Eve, to be at Glenties fair early next day, where he wanted to buy a slip of a pig. He drew upon a light that it surprised him to see in the old scalan on the southwest side of Dunnasalagh hill. Great was his surprise when, coming near the old Mass Rock of that territory – Rock that hadn't spread the news for thirty-five years before, since the new chapel was built at Kilclooney – he saw the rock altar laid out for Mass, the candles lit, and a priest in his vestments standing by, as if he had sent a messenger for something and was awaiting his return.

Though he thought it queer, the Gweebarra man believed it was some strange emergency whereby the priest had to say Mass in the middle of the night, and say it there. Taking off his hat and coming closer, he knelt on the heather, close to the altar, and the priest, coming to him, asked if he could serve Mass. 'In my own kind of way, yes,' said the man. 'They call on me sometimes to do it at the Station house.' At the same time he was staring hard at a scar on the left side of the priest's face, reaching from the top of his head till it disappeared down under his jaw. 'Thanks be to the Lord!' said the priest. 'I have been a long time waiting for you. Come forward, and we'll begin.'

And they did. When the Mass was finished, the Gweebarra man, as he was used to help pack up the Mass things at the Station, made an offer to do the same now. 'Don't bother,' said the priest. 'Go ahead with your journey and God go with you! I'll not forget you,' he added, 'for you have done me a greater service than you know.'

Wondering why the simple serving of Mass for a short-handed priest should be regarded so highly the man went on to Glenties, purchased his little pig, and on his way home, carrying the pig in a bag on his back, called for a drink of milk at a house in Dunnasalagh, where they made him sit and eat supper. At the supper, he asked the people the reason for the priest saying Mass at the *scalan* up the hill, in the middle of last night.

His question dumbfounded them; and then he told them his experience, describing the great scar that was on the priest's face. 'Well, well, well!' said the man of the house, 'that's the most extraordinary thing I've heard in a long while. It has been five and thirty years since Mass was said at that *scalan*, and with us it has the name of being haunted – ever since Friar O'Boyle died five and fifty years before that again. The friar all his latter days carried a great scar on the left side of his face from the cut of a soldier's sword, once that the redcoats cornered and nearly caught him when he made his home in a sheep's craw on the north side of Sliabh Mor.' The old people maintained that the light which people had been used to seeing in the *scalan*, and its name of being haunted, was by reason the friar (God ease him!) must have died with a Mass on his soul that he left unsaid!

From that day forward, there was never more a light seen in the *scalan* on Dunnasalagh.

Many of the apparitions of priests have been explained in

this fashion; that they come back after death to atone for having neglected to say a Mass that had been requested of them.

The Ghost on the Hill

For many years a lonely road near Strokestown, Co. Roscommon, was haunted by the figure of a man carrying a large object on his back.

The story goes back to the Great Famine of 1847, to an Ireland stricken by hunger and stalked by death; to an Ireland of great mansions set in spacious parklands and of tiny roadside thatched hovels; to a land in which travel, for some, meant fine carriages and spirited horses, and to others, slow leisurely trips by canal barge to distant Dublin.

It is the canal barge of the period which features indirectly in this legend of Roscommon, for it was in a desperate effort to reach Killashee in Co. Longford, from where he intended to take the barge on the first stage of a journey to America, that the unfortunate man whose ghost is said to wander the lonely road at dead of night lost his life.

Among the fine houses of the district were a mansion built by Lord Hartland and, near Ballinderry, Hollywell House, where the famous eighteenth-century beauties, the Gunning sisters, lived, but it was from one of the lowly homesteads of the area that the man in this local story came.

At that time, in those hard years immediately after the famine, many of the stricken people emigrated, starting their journey from Killashee.

A man named Sean Burke, from a district called Rossaun, penniless and debilitated after the long, hungry years made up his mind to join the rest of the emigrants and find a better life for himself across the Atlantic. Despite his poor physical condition, he set off, full of hope, for Killashee.

Burke had no food for the journey, but he knew of a neighbour who had ample supplies and decided to call in on his way and request enough provisions to keep him going for a while at least. To his dismay, however, the neighbour would only give him food in exchange for a large round stone, which he knew was in Burke's house, and which he realised would be most useful to him for grinding corn.

Burke, knowing of no other way to get the necessary food, and despite his weak condition, returned to his own abandoned home and got the coveted stone. Hoisting it on to his back, he set off once again for the neighbour's house, but he had not got very far before the effort overcame him and he sank down exhausted on the ground, the huge stone thudding on to the roadway beside him. With no one to come to his assistance, Sean Burke died of hunger on the spot, a pathetic would-be emigrant who never made it to the canal barge at Killashee.

It was the ghost of this tragic victim of Ireland's grim years that was said to have been seen frequently on the road where he died, a grisly reminder of one man's sad fate at a time of national sadness.

Ghosts of the Dublin Liberties

The ghost of Narcissus Marsh, poring over an ancient volume in the library he gave to Dublin; the tragic ghost of Swift stalking the corridors of the old hospital he claimed Dublin so badly needed; the ghosts of Stella and Vanessa, maybe, in the shadows of some dark buttress of St Patrick's or, on the ground that was Faddle Alley, the ghost of blind Michael Moran, who was to become the balladeer Zozimus: the ghosts of industrious Huguenots, who once walked, naked, in protest through its cobbled streets. . . these, and many other ghosts, must haunt the Liberties.

One of the best known stories of the Dublin Liberties is located around Roper's Rest, an old turning off Blackpitts, leading to Love Lane. Here, in 1798, the Liberty Boys drilled, and Jemmy Hope and Emmet frequented the area. It contained the homes of some of the first Quakers to settle in Dublin, including the famous Bewleys, whose unique Oriental Cafes have been for generations such an integral part of Dublin social life.

When darkness settled over Roper's Rest, a headless horseman was said to ride by, a story that brought fear to the hearts

Sunlight filters a zig-zag reflection of the gables of 'Dutch Billys' in the Liberties, but, after dark, in the overcrowded rooms, grandparents in chimney corners told ghost stories to the children, and the shadows of the cobbled streets outside became a frightening world of phantoms.

of local residents whenever a winter dusk had fallen, and prompted many a late traveller to hasten his footsteps homeward.

A couple of years before Thomas Roper was created Viscount Baltinglass, his daughter Ruth was married to Edward Denny at Roper's Rest, where the Ropers had a house. Although the exact connection between Roper's Rest and the headless horseman has never been fully explained, the latter owes its origin to a macabre incident connected with the Roper family, when one of its members died and was left unattended for some days before burial.

Ardee House, the town house of the Earl of Meath, situated in Ardee Street, at the end of the Coombe, long had the reputation of being haunted. Built in 1719, it passed into the hands of the Purser family and eventually became a nurse's home for the Coombe Hospital. It was demolished in 1943.

One of the most reliable testimonies on the hauntings comes from the last stage of its history, when it was a nurses' home, and is recorded by a nurse who later became the distinguished popular novelist, Annie M. P. Smithson.

That the former home of the Earl of Meath was haunted was firmly believed by those nurses who were Miss Smithson's contemporaries there, an opinion to which she herself subscribed unashamedly, and certain parts of the old house were avoided if possible, especially by young nurses on night duty. It was generally conceded that the epicentre of the haunting was the bathroom. Many stories were whispered over furtive cups of tea, but doubtless many of these were figments of stressed imaginations, understandable in a house that had borne silent witness of two centuries of living.

The Coonian Poltergeist

Poltergeists, those strange disembodied spirits who never assume tangible shape but who make their presence felt by such disturbances as the banging of doors, the ringing of bells, the moving and throwing of small objects, and other such manifestations, some of them dangerous but many merely mischievous, sometimes take possession of a house, or attach themselves to a particular family, frequently for no known reason.

In his *Ghost Book*, the late Sir Shane Leslie, who maintained a life-long interest in the paranormal, recorded a remarkable poltergeist that haunted a house at Coonian, near Brookborough, in Co. Fermanagh.

The house, in which it was said that a pensioner had once been murdered, changed hands several times, with suspicious rapidity. One family, indeed, spent only one night under its roof and then sold it. The real trouble began when their successors, a family named Murphy, moved in.

The Coonian poltergeist was nothing if not versatile, and it appears to have been gifted with a vast repertoire. It snored. It emitted noises that appeared to come from far underground. It took human shape under the sheets of a bed. It pulled the bedclothes off members of the unfortunate Murphy family. It made a sound like the kicking of a horse. It hissed and whistled and manifested itself in many other amazing ways. It could even tap out tunes, and two of its favourite numbers were 'Boyne Water' and 'The Soldier's Song.'

The Murphy family were not the only people to experience the strange antics of their unwanted house guest. Many others were present in the house when the poltergeist set about its disturbances. Three priests tried to exorcise it, and it was thought to be of diabolical origin.

As well as being gifted in the variety of its performances, the poltergeist apparently was endowed with an intelligence, for it was able to answer correctly questions put to it. This it did by means of tapping.

The Murphy family eventually could take no more of these weird happenings in their home. They emigrated to the United States and were no longer troubled.

Exorcism at Burren

The strange stories that for many years centred around a lonely farmhouse at Burren, Derrygarry, on the Cavan-Leitrim border, had their origin in the middle of the nineteenth century and embraced romance, a curse, a poltergeist and, finally, an exorcism.

The house was the home of a well-to-do farmer named Owen McLavey, his wife and young family, and life in the comfortable, single-story dwelling was normal enough until McLavey became involved with a local girl. She became pregnant and claimed that McLavey was responsible, demanding that he either marry her or accompany her to America. When he refused, she cursed him and called on the devil to avenge the wrong which she claimed he had done.

Shortly afterwards, the girl left for America, and the farmer, doubtless glad to see her go, must have been further relieved when news reached the district that she had been drowned at sea.

McLavey's relief, however, was short-lived, for soon afterwards a series of strange happenings occurred in his home, affecting not only himself but also members of his family.

What happened seemed to be the work of a particularly vicious poltergeist. When the family went to bed at night, the bedclothes were regularly whipped off the beds by an unseen hand and torn to shreds. Doors became jammed and then loosened just as inexplicably. Kitchen pots boiled over, scalding anyone who happened to be near.

On top of all this, articles were flung through the air, sometimes striking members of the family, and strange noises that could not be accounted for were heard in the night. After six months of continual persecution, the family finally contacted the local clergy.

In a report of the strange story that has become part of the folklore of the district, published in the *Evening Press* in February 1973, a local woman whose grandfather had taken a priest to the McLavey home remembered from her childhood his account of what had happened when they arrived at the haunted farmhouse.

The curate would not enter the house until his parish priest arrived but stood outside waiting.

'When the parish priest arrived,' she said, 'he told my grandfather and Father McGovern to wait outside the house. He put on a stole and opened his prayer book. He began reciting prayers and strolled through the house, praying in every room.

He remained doing this,' the woman said, 'for almost one hour.'

It was then that Father McGovern, standing at the door, felt a force of some kind pushing him out of the doorway.

The parish priest was pale and shaking when he came out of the house, and he called for Owen McLavey who was nearby. He told him he had banished the spirit from the house, but it was still present in the environs of the farmhouse. The priest told McLavey never to build in any direction from the house or the spirit would be back.

Owen McLavey continued to live in the farmhouse for the rest of his life, and there was never any repetition of the frightening occurrences, as he rigidly honoured the priest's warning about extending the building in any direction.

For many years afterwards, however, the little house at Burren retained its grim reputation in the neighbourhood and local people avoided passing it unless they had to, especially after nightfall. It eventually became vacant and remained so for many years.

The Clongowes Spectre

Two miles north of the little village of Clane in Co. Kildare, and not very far from Bodenstown Churchyard, the burial place of Wolfe Tone, one meets impressive gateways opening on to a long tree-lined avenue. The ancient building at the end of the avenue is Clongowes Wood College, the educational establishment run by the Jesuit Fathers, exclusive, expensive, dubbed at times 'the Eton of Ireland'.

James Joyce, when he was a pupil at Clongowes, must have been very aware of the eerie stories told about the old house, for, in the autobiographical *A Portrait of the Artist as a Young Man*, he vividly describes the terror of the new boy (himself) lying in a strange bed in a vast dormitory on his lonely first night who, when the prefect had turned off the lights and left, became suddenly petrified with fear engendered by the stories already whispered to him.

There was a phantom black dog here, they had told him, 'with eyes as big as carriage-lamps', who roamed the corridors of the college by night, the ghost of a murderer, they said.

And another old legend of Clongowes tormented the young Joyce as he lay sleepless in the hopeless darkness of the alien dormitory, the enduring ghost story of Clongowes, still recounted nervously by the domestic staff and at the hearth-stones of the Co. Kildare countryside. It told of women here, long ago, disturbed at night by a dreadful visitation, the arrival in the entrance hall below of a phantom in a marshal's uniform, with an ashen face and a great wound in his side.

The school, opened by the Jesuit Fathers in 1814, was built around the original castle, which had been the home of the Wogan-Browne family since 1667. It was in the ancient hall, one evening, that two sisters of the family, to their terror, saw their soldier brother stagger in through the great hall door. At the time he was serving as a marshal in the Austrian army, not the only member of the family to make distinguished careers in continental armies.

The two girls saw that their brother's hands and uniform were bloodstained, and, despite their fear they followed him as he lurched up the stairs. At the door of his own bedroom, he vanished.

Suspecting that this terrifying apparition indicated that their brother had been killed in the war, the sisters spread the news around the neighbourhood, and, so sure were they of the meaning of the fearsome encounter, that they even held a 'wake'. Several weeks passed before their fears were confirmed, when they were officially informed that Marshal Wogan-Browne had died in battle at Prague on the very day he had appeared in his old home.

The castle remained in the Wogan-Browne family until General Michael Wogan-Browne, an aide-de-camp to the King of Saxony, sold the property to the Society of Jesus.

Ghosts of Skryne

Some ill-starred buildings have a number of ghosts attached to them. There are, for example, the many ghosts of historic Glamis Castle, the ancestral Scottish home of the Bowes-Lyon

Skryne Castle, Co. Meath. . . with its echoes of the eighteenth century tragedy of Lilith Palmerston, surviving in the legend of a ghostly woman and shrieks in the darkness. (Photo: the author)

family, one of whose daughters was destined to become a Queen of England.

And there is the even more dramatic case of the famous hauntings attributed to the notorious Borley Rectory, near Long Melford, on the borders of Essex and Suffolk, which earned such a long history of the supernatural that the well-known psychical researcher, Harry Price, in the first book that recorded his investigations there, dubbed it 'The Most Haunted House in England.'

Glamis is content with the unfading bloodstain said to be the relic of the murder of Duncan by Macbeth, a monster, a secret room, a grey lady and a few others, but Borley has a record of strange happenings and apparitions recurring frequently from the time it was built in 1863 until it was mysteriously burned to the ground in 1939, an event which had been predicted during a seance in the house a short time earlier. Its ghosts ran the entire gamut of the supernatural, from the nun-like figure seen on the 'Nun's Walk', to flying bricks, phantom coaches, mysterious footsteps and conversations, messages on walls and bells that rang without the aid of any human agency.

Ireland, too, has houses that can claim several ghosts. One of these is located close to what must be, in another way, the most haunted hill in the country, the historic Hill of Tara in Co. Meath, once the religious, political and cultural capital of Ireland and the residence of the High King.

On the slopes of the hill, at a spot called Skryne, or Cnoc Ghuile, the Hill of Weeping, stands Skryne Castle, built in 1172 and rebuilt early in the nineteenth century, close to where a rebellious Fianna fought in the battle of Cowra. The stories that have been told about it embrace the ghosts of a nun, a woman in white and a tall man with a dog, together with weird shrieks at night.

In 1740 the castle was owned and occupied by a Sir Bromley Casway, who had in his care a ward named Lilith Palmerston. The girl spent some time in Dublin, but then returned to live with her guardian at Skryne.

The story has all the ingredients of Victorian melodrama, and indeed, may well have inspired some of the romantic novelists of the following century, for Lilith's beauty attracted the unwelcomed attentions of a wealthy squire who lived close by. This man, Phelim Sellers, attempted to woo the young girl, and when his advances were spurned, he did not accept his rejection but rather renewed his efforts in amorous supplication, with an ardour that demanded some action on the part of his victim.

Lilith, therefore, in order to escape Sellers and his attentions, decided to return to Dublin. But news of her intended departure must have been conveyed to the would-be suitor, for, on the night before she was due to leave Skryne, Sellers went to the castle, forced an entry and made his way to the girl's room. This swashbuckling effort ended in tragedy, for when the girl still resisted him the squire strangled her, and was hanged in Galway City for the crime.

The shrieks heard in the castle at dead of night may perhaps be those of the unfortunate Lilith Palmerston, spanning two centuries, just as it may well be her ghost that takes the form of the mysterious woman in white who has been seen running through the grounds, clutching her throat.

Glencairn's Girl in White

On the banks of the lovely Blackwater, in County Waterford, three miles from Lismore, stands Glencairn Abbey, a gracious old mansion with a ghost story of its own. Now a Cistercian convent, it was, in the past, a private residence, said to have been haunted by the ghost of a young girl in white.

In the middle of the nineteenth century Glencairn was the home of the Bushe family, and it was when a Colonel Bushe, having served for many years abroad, came back to Ireland to settle down in the old family home, that he found a disquieting state of affairs in the old house.

Rumour had spread that Glencairn was haunted, and this influenced the local people to such an extent that the servants refused to sleep in the house and instead installed themselves in outbuildings.

Despite Colonel Bushe's pleadings, the servants would not move indoors, and as this was somewhat inconvenient for the owner of Glencairn he proceeded to engage servants from places beyond the reach of local rumour. When these arrived, however, they too quickly expressed a wish to move into the outbuildings.

Pressed by their employer as to the reason for their unease in the house, they confessed to hearing footsteps that could not be accounted for, and said that they were frequently kept awake at night by noises coming from the attics and upper rooms. One servant claimed to have caught sight of a young girl dressed in white, who vanished almost at once.

Determined to get to the bottom of the mystery, Colonel Bushe sent for an old friend, a Mr Seigne, who was interested in supernatural manifestations, and arranged for him to stay as his guest at Glencairn.

Seigne was not long in residence at the Abbey when both he and his host were awakened at night by the sound of footsteps and the noise of doors opening and closing, coming it seemed. . . just as the servants had claimed. . . from the upper regions of the house. Despite an intensive room-to-room search by the two men, nothing by way of explanation was revealed.

Presently Seigne left for home, and with all the servants now installed in the outbuildings, Colonel Bushe was sleeping in the house alone. One night, shortly after his friend's departure, he was awakened by the sound of footsteps. His bedroom door opened and a young girl entered and stood in front of his bed. Just before she vanished he noticed that she appeared to have a wound in her breast. He then heard footsteps going upstairs and the sound of a door opening and closing.

Next morning Colonel Bushe went up to the attic, and although it appeared to be undisturbed he determined to carry out an exhaustive search, feeling that somewhere in this room lay the secret of the hauntings. Sifting through the contents of the room, he eventually found a small wooden box. Inside was a sealed metal box and a parchment. The parchment stated that the metal box contained the heart of a young girl. . . the daughter of a previous owner of the Abbey. . . who had died in Rome and who wished that her heart might be buried at Glencairn.

Armed with this information, Colonel Bushe began a search through old family documents, and among some records of fifty years earlier, discovered more about the girl, whose apparition, he had little doubt, he had seen in his bedroom.

The girl had apparently fallen into ill health, and it had been decided that she should be sent abroad to recover. She moved from one place to another in Europe, but, despite the sunshine and the change of air, her condition failed to improve. She had reached Rome when her illness took a further sharp decline, and she expressed the wish to be sent home to Glencairn, the old house on the Blackwater that she loved so much. It was decided to accede to her request, but, before she could be moved, she died. Her last request was that her heart be buried at Glencairn, and before she was interred in the English cemetery in Rome, her heart was removed from her body and placed in a casket in order to be brought back to Ireland.

Colonel Bushe, despite further research, could not find any explanation as to why the casket had not been buried, or why it had been left in the attic at Glencairn.

He sent for Mr Seigne again, and when his friend arrived, together they opened the metal box and in it, wrapped in yellow silk, found an embalmed human heart. They buried the tragic relic in a remote part of the garden, telling nobody the whereabouts of the spot. There were no further disturbances in the old mansion.

Glencairn Abbey, with its sad mystery, passed out of private ownership at the turn of the century, when it was bought by the Cistercian Order.

The Aughavanagh Hangman

Hikers in the Wicklow mountains, or climbers challenging nearby Lugnaquilla, may be familiar with one of the most popular youth hostels in this sprawling county that is a paradise for lovers of the outdoors. This is the old hostel situated in the heart of wild and beautiful country at Aughavanagh.

The Irish Youth Hostel Organisation, An Oige, purchased the building in 1943, and since then young holidaymakers and week-enders, tired from treking the twisting white mountain roads, have stayed there on overnight visits. Yet, many of those seeking the peace of its dormitories have been unaware that it is the setting for one of the most bizarre ghost stories to be found in Ireland. The Aughavanagh hostel is said to be haunted by the ghost of a hangman.

The old building, like the military road that leads to it over the mountains from picturesque Glenmalure, dates from the late eighteenth century, when Michael Dwyer, the leader of the 1798 insurrection, sought refuge in this almost impenetrable natural fortress of wild hill and woodland. In their efforts to capture Dwyer and his men, the British built the long brave road that crosses the Dublin and Wicklow mountains to Laragh, then to Glenmalure, and onwards to Aughavanagh. At Glenmalure, they erected Drumgoff Barracks, now a great formidable ruin, and, at Aughavanagh, the building that is now the youth hostel. Both were part of a chain of military block-houses, a determined official plan to bring the redoubtable Dwyer and his followers to their knees.

One of the most terrifying characters of the period was the hangman, a giant named Hempenstall. An object of hate and legend, it was said of him that he was so tall that he could make himself a human gallows, by hoising his unfortunate victims over his shoulder and walking about until they died, a practice that earned him the title 'the walking hangman'.

But retribution lay in store for Hempenstall, and his own end was every bit as violent as those he had for so long doled out to many others. A group of survivors of the '98 rebellion lay in wait for him at the gateway of the blockhouse in Aughavanagh and killed him on the spot.

And it is there, at the gateway familiar to so many visitors to today's hostel, that there have been frequent reports of the apparition of a frightening figure, over seven feet in height. . . the ghost of the hangman Hempenstall.

When the old building ceased to have any use as a military blockhouse, it was used for some time as a shooting lodge by Charles Stewart Parnell. After Parnell's death, it was bought by John Redmond, the leading Parnellite, who used it as a residence.

The old gateway still stands today, in its remote and peaceful setting, much as it was on the turbulent evening when the notorious 'walking hangman' met rough justice at the hands of men so many of whose friends and comrades had found no mercy from Hempenstall.

Vengeance of Olocher

It was a dark night in the old Dublin district known as 'Hell.' Through an alleyway black as pitch the figure of a woman flitted silently. Unheard. . . but not unseen. . . she passed, a fleeting silhouette against a lighted window. Next moment, her terrified screams shattered the silence, petrifying into numb horror all who were within earshot in the congested houses around.

The incident was just another chapter in the paralysing reign of terror that made the streets and alleys of Old Dublin a place of dread throughout the long, dark months of one fear-ridden winter.

Lone women became the subjects of savage attacks. These came unexpectedly, always at night, and in Dublin homes and taverns it was whispered that the attacker was a big black pig. . . and they called it the 'Dolocher.'

It had all started some time earlier when one of the most notorious criminals ever to be thrown behind bars in the formidable old Black Dog Prison committed suicide. This man's name was Olocher, and he had been sentenced to death for the murder of a woman.

With Olocher cheating the gallows at the last minute in so dramatic a fashion, it was probably inevitable that rumour should run rife, but an incident that took place in the Black Dog Prison the night after Olocher's suicide struck terror into the entire town.

A sentry who had been on guard in the prison was found unconscious and very badly mauled. When he regained consciousness, he said that he had been attacked by a big black pig.

News of this strange affair had barely filtered out of the prison precincts when the incident was followed by something even stranger and more bizarre. Another sentry simply vanished into thin air.

This man's gun was found behind the sentry-box with his clothes draped around it. . . but of the man himself there was not a trace. It was immediately assumed that he had been devoured by the black pig.

The town was soon in ferment. Fear stalked the streets after

'Come home before dark, or the Dolocher will get you. . .' a fearsome warning to youngsters of another era.

dark, and most people, except the foolhardy few, avoided going abroad after nightfall. Then the rumours began to spread, and one report followed another. . . all from women claiming to have encountered the black pig.

Soon it became apparent that most of the reports were genuine, and not mere figments of imagination inspired by the strange occurrences at the Black Dog Prison. Several more women were attacked by the black pig, and the slightest shuffle in a silent street sent people hurrying for shelter. Dublin by night became a ghost town.

It was generally accepted that the black pig was the ghost of Olocher, on a rampage of vengeance, and the terrible thing that stalked the alleyways under the cloak of darkness became known as the 'Dolocher.'

But that long, fear-ridden winter passed, and with it passed the 'Dolocher'. The attacks ceased and the town breathed freely again.

There were recurrences of the attacks the following winter, and reports suggest that the mystery was solved when a blacksmith, returning home from a tavern, borrowed a woman's cloak to protect him from the rain; he was attacked but he overpowered his assailant, who turned out to be the sentry from the prison who had so mysteriously disappeared. He had clad himself in the skin of a large black pig.

The eerie tale of the 'Dolocher' is part of Dublin folklore. Ghost or psychopath? The answer remains hidden in the stones of 'Hell'.

The Wizard Earl

There is an alien, almost Transylvanian, atmosphere about the legends attached to one of Ireland's most haunted castles, that squat, massive pile of Kilkea, that rears its castellated turrets high over the green plains of County Kildare, near the town of Castledermot.

The castle, now an excellent luxury hotel, is redolent of 'old, forgotten far-off things and battles long ago' and for many centuries stories have been whispered of strange apparitions in the

Kilkea Castle, Castledermot, Co. Kildare, where Garrett Og Fitzgerald practised the Black Arts, and from which the ghost of the Wizard Earl rides out at night, bound for the haunted Rath of Mullaghmast. (Photo: Bord Failte)

castle and neighbourhood, the eerie clash of steel upon steel on lofty battlements, of phantom warriors, re-enacting old skirmishes on history-soaked ground.

In a way, Kilkea, with its 'haunted wing', is, indeed, the Glamis of Ireland. Linked in legend with the awe-inspiring Rath of Mullaghmast, a few miles away, its past is dominated, however, by the shadow of the Wizard Earl.

It was Garrett Og Fitzgerald who earned this title, for he was said to practise black magic, and there is a room at Kilkea which, according to legend, he used for this purpose.

The Fitzgeralds, the Earls of Kildare, are first recorded as having an association with Kilkea in 1244, about seventy years after the castle had been built either by Hugh de Lacy or by a Norman invader named Sir Walter Riddlesford.

Few families are more tenaciously entangled with Irish history than the Fitzgeralds, and Kilkea supplied the formidable backdrop to much of their activities, as years drifted into decades and decades into centuries.

The castle's past speaks of close links with Silken Thomas, who, acting as Lord Deputy of Ireland, threw down his sword in rebellion against the crown in Dublin's St Mary's Abbey, when duped into believing that his father had been executed in the Tower of London, and who was himself later to die at Tyburn.

The old stronghold has associations, too, with Cardinal Rinuccini, with the 1798 informer Thomas Reynolds, and with the gallant Lord Edward Fitzgerald. It was restored in 1849, although much of the original building remains.

Kilkea, then, is surely a place in which it is easy to believe in ghosts, where vibrations of a stormy past must be embedded still in time-worn walls.

While the stories centring around Kilkea are many, the most persistent legend is, inevitably, that woven about its Wizard Earl, who is said to sleep under a spell in the Rath of Mullaghmast, from which he rides out sometimes at dead of night to gallop across the windswept plains of the Curragh on a magnificent white horse shod with silver shoes.

The Rath, near Ballitore, was the scene of the massacre of the chieftains of Laois and Offaly in 1577 by the English.

The Room at Maynooth

One of the strangest and most bizarre of all stories of super-natural manifestation in Ireland is that attached to St Patrick's College in Maynooth, Co. Kildare.

St Patrick's was founded under an Act of the Irish Parliament in 1795. Starting with a mere forty students and ten professors, it expanded rapidly, and has for long been the principal training centre for Catholic priests in Ireland and a constituent college of the National University of Ireland.

The original college building stands on the site of an earlier college founded by the Earl of Kildare in the sixteenth century, close to Maynooth Castle, the ancient seat of the Fitzgeralds.

The story of the Maynooth haunting dates from the 1840s and is centred in the House of Rhetoric, a building to the left of the main courtyard. The top floor of this building consisted mainly of bedrooms for the students, a use which it serves to the present day.

The eerie events began on this floor, when a student was assigned the second room on the corridor, Room No. 2. The youth committed suicide, reportedly with a razor, close to the single window in the room.

Some time later, a second student was allotted Room No. 2, and apparently acting under some irresistible compulsion, did exactly what his unfortunate predecessor had done.

These two events were, understandably, attributed by the college authorities to nothing more than a very tragic coincidence, and, in time, a third student was sent to occupy the room. This man nearly suffered the same fate. He was almost overcome by a compulsion to take his own life and only escaped whatever strange power had gripped him by throwing himself desperately through the window. Although be broke some bones in the fall, he escaped with his life.

After this third incident, although it had not the tragic outcome of the two that had gone before it, the college governors must have felt that some attention should be paid to Room No. 2. A priest volunteered to occupy the room and to keep vigil in it. No record has been released of what happened to him during the night, but it is accepted that, although he survived, his hair had turned white by morning.

It is part of the legend of Maynooth's haunted room that students at one time could point out bloodstains on the wall and a footprint in the wood. Whatever the veracity of such embellishments, it is a verifiable fact that a resolution passed by the college trustees on 23 October 1860 read:

'That the President be authorised to convert Room No. 2 on the top corridor of Rhetoric House into an Oratory of St Joseph and to fit up an oratory of St Aloysius in the prayer hall of the junior students.'

Whether the directive about the prayer hall had any connection with the events in the room on the top floor is not recorded, but the corridor wall of Room No. 2 was demolished, the window blocked up and a shrine to St Joseph installed. As such, it exists to the present day.

So widespread is the story of Maynooth's haunted room that the House of Rhetoric has a regular stream of curious visitors, and it is not difficult to gain admission to what is now the Oratory of St Joseph.

While details vary according to the teller, perhaps the most reliable account of the affair is to be found in Father Denis Meehan's book, *Window on Maynooth*. He writes:

The basic details of the story have doubtless some foundation in fact, and it is safe to assume that something very unpleasant did occur. The suicide (or suicides), in so far as one can deduce from the oral traditions that remain, seem to have taken place in the period 1842-48. A few colourful adjuncts, that used to form part of the stock-in-trade of the storyteller are passing out of memory now.

AT THE MID HOUR OF NIGHT

At the mid hour of night, when stars are weeping, I fly
To the lone vale we loved, when life shone warm in thine eye;
And I think oft, if spirits can steal from the regions of air,
To revisit past scenes of delight, thou wilt come to me there,
And tell me our love is remember'd, even in the sky!

Then I sing the wild song 'twas once such pleasure to hear,
When our voices, commingling, breathed, like one, on the ear;

And, as Echo far off through the vale my sad orison rolls,
I think, O my love! 'tis thy voice, from the Kingdom of Souls,
Faintly answering still the notes that once were so dear.

Thomas Moore

The Dean's Ghost

If the Dublin Liberties were to yield a ghost, and there must
be many ghosts in those crowded, teeming streets in the shadow
of St Patrick's, the most likely would be that of Jonathan Swift,
author of *Gullivers's Travels*, crusader behind the Drapier mask,
satirist, wit, crank, who came a reluctant Dean to St Patrick's
and was at first loathed by the people of the streets around,
but who remained for thirty-two years in their midst and
became so loved by them that they were known to escort him,
with cheers and bands, to St Patrick's Close. And he, in turn,
grew to love the occupants of the fetid, congested, crumbling
homes of this heart of Dublin.

There are many places where the wraith of Swift might be
expected to walk: Marsh's Library; Newlands House in Clondalkin, where he was a visitor; Glasnevin, and the site of the
house called Delville, where his friends, the Delanys, lived.

Is there also a quiet corner in the village of Laracor, in Co.
Meath, where he once tried his hand at market-gardening,
which harbours the ghost of Swift, or does he still talk at Celbridge, in Co. Kildare, the poignant, tragic setting of his last,
gruff encounter with the celebrated Vanessa? Or, on some
moonlit night, is it the Dean who is seen in Phoenix Park, at
the spot where once, during a thunderstorm, he married a
young man and woman under the shelter of a tree?

Not surprisingly, perhaps, the place most often said to be
haunted by Swift is St Patrick's, the psychiatric hospital he
founded in James's Street, even at a time when he himself was
already in that dark tunnel that was to engulf him over the
final decade of his life.

Stories have long persisted that the ghost of Swift is seen in
St Patrick's, and, over many years, patients and medical staff
alike have subscribed to the evidence. The oldest psychiatric

hospital in Ireland, and, indeed, among the oldest in the world, its time-worn buildings, with their long corridors and ancient rooms, are still permeated with much of the past and especially with the memory of the devoted genius who fathered the hospital.

St Patrick's became Swift's main interest during the last years of his life, and was endowed under the terms of his will, a document couched with the barb, so typical of the Drapier, that no city needed a psychiatric hospital as sorely as did Dublin.

The Dean's wishes were fulfilled when St Patrick's opened its doors in 1745, ironically, that same year when his shrunken corpse was carried by night for furtive burial under the great bulk of the cathedral which he was forever to make uniquely his own.

Ghosts of St Stephen's Green

The spectral figure of a tragic girl flitting through a stately Georgian town house; a cross that appears each Holy Week in the pane of a window; the ghost of a child haunting a hotel bedroom that was once part of her home; these are some of the supernatural manifestations recorded about St Stephen's Green in Dublin.

Despite the ravages of time and the developer, its finely proportioned squares remain one of the most attractive features of Georgian Dublin. And, of all these, the best known and finest is what Dubliners familiarly call 'The Green'.

And, indeed, St Stephen's Green, having weathered the years for as long as it has done, certainly deserves its share of ghosts. This once unenclosed common owned by the Corporation, was first laid out in building lots in 1663, the 'Green' in the centre later being surrounded by a ditch and a low wall which, after the Union, was levelled and drained.

Early in the nineteenth century, a distinguished English visitor, a Devonshire barrister named Sir John Carr, came to Dublin.

He admired St Stephen's Green, 'a fine meadow, walled and

planted with a double row of trees', and liked its stately houses, although he expressed his distaste for the ditch that then surrounded it, 'the receptacle of dead cats and dogs', and thought that this prevented the Green from being 'one of the most magnificent in Europe'.

Today, one of the most impressive houses on St Stephen's Green is the Department of Foreign Affairs, or Iveagh House, once the residence of the Earl of Iveagh, and given by the Guinness family to the nation in recent times. It is this house that holds the tradition of the mysterious cross in the window.

For many years a familiar sight in Dublin each Holy Thursday was the gathering together of large crowds by the railings of the Green, opposite Iveagh House, in the hope of catching a glimpse of the cross that was said to appear on one pane of glass in a particular window.

The most common explanation of the phenomenon was that a servant girl, a Catholic in a Protestant household, had lain dying in the room and had been refused a priest by her employer, who, catching the girl saying the Rosary, had grasped the beads and thrown them through the window. Hence, claimed the Dublin believers, the cross appeared on the window every Holy Thursday.

There were others, however, who thought that the appearance of the cross possibly had a connection with the death of the Archbishop of Cashel who was said to have been murdered in 1583 on the spot where the house was later built.

Looking over the treetops of the Green is Dublin's internationally famous Shelbourne Hotel, which acquired and has retained its reputation despite William Makepiece Thackeray's reference in 1842, when he was writing his *Irish Sketch Book*, to this 'respectable old edifice much frequented by families from the country'. In spite of its 'ruin and liberality' he was impressed by its public rooms, food and a friendly waiter named Pat.

A ghostly experience in the hotel was recorded in the 1960s by an American investigator, Hans Holzer, who included it later in his book *The Lively Ghosts of Ireland*.

Mr Holzer and his wife, with a woman 'medium' who was helping them with their research in Ireland, stayed at the Shelbourne during a visit to Dublin.

During the stay, the friend occupied a small room on the top

Do the ghosts of Buck Whaley and the Sham Squire still frequent the quiet pathways of St Stephen's Green? This photograph, looking down fashionable Grafton Street, was taken on a forgotten day before the Boer War disrupted its empirical Victorian complacency.

floor, which she claimed was haunted by the ghost of a little girl named Mary Masters, who spoke to her.

No explanation for this apparition was forthcoming, but the hotel has a long history and perhaps somewhere in its past lies the story of little Mary Masters, perhaps back in the years before the Shelbourne was formed from four separate houses bought by Martin Burke in 1824.

Close to the Shelbourne Hotel stands another house that has a ghost story of its own, the echo of a long-ago tragedy dating from before the house itself was built.

In 1760 the fashionable Green was taking shape, and new houses were built around the ditch that had so repulsed Sir John Carr. Lord Joselyn's town mansion on the west side of the Green was already occupied, but beside it another house was in the course of construction. The foundations had already been laid, and, after heavy rainfall, had become waterlogged. Here, one morning, the body of a young woman was found, and later identified as one of a group of ladies of the town who were familiar paraders along the Green, close to Cuffe Street.

Two years later, the house was completed and became the property of Francis Sadleir of Tipperary. In the years that followed, the property changed hands many times, and some of those who occupied it told of uncanny experiences, the sensing of a presence, a feeling that someone was watching, or standing close by.

Dublin's most famous square, in many ways the very heart of the city, is haunted by many ghosts besides those here recorded. . . Martin Burke, who set the tone of the Green when he gave it its famous hotel. . . the Sham Squire, hurrying to a secret tryst with a Castle agent. . . and Buck Whaley, said to have jumped on horseback from a first-floor window, and who played handball against the walls of Jerusalem just for a wager.

The Ghost of Loftus Hall

Few counties of Ireland are richer in folklore than Co. Wexford, and few parts of that county are permeated more densely by echoes of the past than its straggling south-easterly limit, the

Hook peninsula. And, here, one of the more enduring legends is that of the lovely girl said to haunt the mansion known as Loftus Hall.

On the last stretch of the drive to the fishing village of Slade, where the Tower of Hook lighthouse stands sentinel on a promontory, the road is straight and narrow before it enters the village, and here, on the right, as one approaches Slade, stands Loftus Hall.

Loftus Hall today houses a community of nuns, a tranquil imposing place ideally suited to its present purpose, but it was built in less settled days and at least one of its occupants of the past had her share of frustration and sorrow. It was her ghost that was said to glide silently through the old rooms that had witnessed her unhappiness, until they were exorcised by the parish priest of the district.

Built on the site of a fort that dated from Cromwellian times, the mansion fell into the hands of a member of the Irish Parliament, Charles Tottenham, who earned the title 'Tottenham of the Boots' because of a mad dash he once made to the College Green parliament to give a casting vote.

If Tottenham was devoted to his parliamentary duties in Dublin, when he was at home in Wexford he was equally devoted to his role as host at the fine old mansion on the peninsula. A gregarious man, he liked to throw parties, at which he could fill the house with friends and neighbours.

A most presentable young man attended one of these gatherings at Loftus Hall, and before the evening was over had discovered for himself that the house held an attraction other than Tottenham's good wine and the witty conversation of the guests. The bonus attraction for the visitor was, in fact, Charles Tottenham's daughter, and he immediately fell in love with her, and she with him.

An affair started between them, but, for reasons of his own, Tottenham did not approve, and, when a wedding appeared to be in the offing, he promptly refused to give his permission, despite all the pleadings of his distraught daughter.

The would-be suitor was banished from Loftus Hall, and the girl, pining for her lover, became moody and introspective. When it became apparent that her father would not relent, her depression increased, and her health failed rapidly. Almost before Charles Tottenham realised what his attitude had brought about, his daughter was dead.

Not long after she was buried, whispers spread in the district that her ghost was appearing at the Hall, a slim lovely figure in a white dress that moved silently and gracefully through the old apartments.

Reports of the apparition continued for some considerable time, until, eventually, the parish priest was called upon to conduct an exorcism, which he did, apparently with success.

Another legend of the district concerns the Tower of Hook itself and embodies yet another family 'curse'. It was recorded in depth by Mr and Mrs S. C. Hall during their travels around the country in the middle of the nineteenth century, and found a place in their three-volume work, *Ireland*:

> Tintern Abbey, a few miles south-west of Clonmines, was originally founded by William, Earl Marshal of England, and Earl of Pembroke, who wedded the lady Isabella de Clare, daughter of Earl Strongbow by his second wife, the Princess Eva MacMorough, in whose right he claimed the lordship of Leinster. The Earl, when in great danger at sea, made a vow that, in case he escaped, he would found an abbey on the spot where he landed in safety. His bark sheltered in Bannow bay, and he scrupulously performed his vow by founding this abbey, which he dedicated to the Virgin Mary, and filled with Cistercian monks, whom he brought from Tintern, in Monmouthshire, a monastery that owed its foundation to the house of De Clare.
>
> After the dissolution, the buildings and appurtenances were granted, by Queen Elizabeth, to Sir Anthony Colclough, captain of the band of gentlemen pensioners, to hold *in capite*, at the annual rent of twenty-six shillings and fourpence, Irish money.
>
> The Colcloughs are one of the families that are under 'the curse of fire and water,' said to be common to a few, in England as well as in Ireland, who hold estates once owned by the church. The neighbouring peasantry have a legend, ascribing an evil influence of this sort, partly to this cause, and partly to a tradition that Sir Anthony murdered all the friars he found in the house on taking possession; but chiefly

to the fact of an ancient rath, one of those said to have been frequented by the fairies, having been levelled by Sir Caesar Colclough.

Of this latter gentleman they narrate the following tale: He was engaged to the lovely heiress of Redmond, of the Tower of Hook, and going over to England on a mission that shall be described, the lady promised to burn a light in her chamber to guide him on his return home. Having boasted much of the exploits of the Wexford hurlers to King William, with whom he was intimate, that monarch challenged him to bring over twenty-one men of the county to play a match with the famous hurlers of Cornwall.

Sir Caeser held a grand game at Tintern Abbey, and selecting the best players, took them over to the English court; the king and queen, and a large assemblage of the nobility, witnessed the match. Out of compliment to William, the Irish were provided with yellow sashes, or handkerchiefs, for their waists, from which circumstances Wexfordmen are still often called 'yellow bellies'.

The Irish were, of course, victors. Colclough, returning in triumph, steered for the Tower of Hook. Here the enraged fairies interposed: they lulled the lady to sleep with their music, and extinguished her constant lamp; her lover was wrecked, and his dead body cast on shore. The disconsolate young heiress, to save the lives of future mariners, converted her father's tower into a lighthouse, which it remains to the present day.

There is another tradition, more reasonable though equally romantic; that the first Colclough was secretary to a nobleman, who obtained the grant. This secretary he sent to the court of Elizabeth, to have the grant ratified; his appearance and address so won upon the virgin queen, that when he returned to Ireland, he found that the deeds conferred the estates upon himself.

Thus, Wexford's historic Hook peninsula cherishes the tragedies of two women, the valiant lady of the lighthouse, whose lover perished because of a fairy curse, and the gentle girl of Loftus Hall, who lost hers through a father's intransigence.

Ghosts of Rathfarnham

It is hardly surprising that a building as old as Rathfarnham Castle, at Rathfarnham, Co. Dublin, is accredited in local gossip with, not one ghost, but several. It is said to have a haunted room and a phantom dog, while one of its gate lodges has long had the reputation of being haunted by a boy.

The castle is situated at the foothills of the Dublin mountains, at the gateway to the sprawling, rugged hill country that spills over Montpellier, where the ruins of the infamous Hell Fire Club stand, and then tumbles in a profusion of heathered bogland across the windswept Featherbed mountain into Wicklow.

It is an historic place, with a long and at times stormy archive of events associated with it. The original castle that stood on the site was the scene of attack and counterattack between warring factions, offering protection to those who occupied it, just as its nearby hills supplied safe retreat for raiders who swooped down to challenge its grim, high walls.

The castle was the residence of Viscount Baltinglass, who lost it, together with his other estates, when he was convicted for his leadership of an insurrection.

A second castle was erected by the Protestant Archbishop of Dublin, its construction being started in 1583 and being mainly completed two years later. Over the following centuries it was considerably enlarged, especially after 1913 when it was bought by the Jesuit Order, who used it as a residence and as a centre for weekend retreats.

Some years ago, during a visit to Rathfarnham Castle, now a Retreat house, I was told by a Jesuit brother that it had indeed, a 'haunted room', but he did not offer to show me the apartment, and no explanation was given as to why it had such a reputation.

Long before the Jesuits came to the castle other stories, however, had sprung up around it. One concerned a tragedy that occurred there in the 1840s, about the same period that the strange stories began to circulate about Maynooth College in Co. Kildare.

The setting for the unfortunate affair was the pond in the grounds of the castle, which can be seen to the present day. In

The ornate entrance hall of Rathfarnham Castle in its Victorian heyday (c. 1897). The castle was built by a Protestant Archbishop of Dublin and later purchased by the Jesuit Order. Upstairs, a haunted room and, in the grounds outside, tragedy at a pond.

the grip of a severe winter, this pond was frozen over, and inevitably attracted a party of hardy skaters. At the height of their fun, however, tragedy struck. The ice on the pond broke, and a man who, a short time before, had arrived at the pond accompanied by a dog, and who had joined in the skating, fell through the ice into the dark water underneath.

Powerless to go to the assistance of their companion, the helpless onlookers saw the dog plunge into the hole in the ice, in a gallant and devoted effort to save his master. Both the man and the dog were drowned.

The courage of the animal so impressed everybody that a monument was later erected by local people to commemorate the dog's bravery. In the years that followed, it became a common belief in Rathfarnham that the ghost of the animal could be seen in the vicinity of the fatal pond, and sometimes, indeed, in other parts of the castle grounds.

The ghost of the boy associated with Rathfarnham Castle does not seem to be connected with the drowning tragedy and is not attached to the main building itself but to a gate lodge at one of the entrances to the extensive grounds. It was believed that the apparition was that of a boy who had been murdered in the little house.

The vast, indomitable bulk of Rathfarnham Castle still looms today on the slopes of the Dublin hills, its time-defying walls silent with their secrets of its chequered past.

The Man in the Cloak

Who is the tall, gaunt man, carrying a light under his left arm, and wearing a long dark cloak, who is said to haunt a lonely country road near the town of Clones in Co. Monaghan?

This is an historic part of west Monaghan. In early Christian times, a monastery was founded in Clones by Saint Tighearnach, who died in the town, which has an ancient sculptured cross and a round tower. The village of Aghnakillagh, two miles to the east, was the birthplace of James Connolly, one of the leaders of the 1916 Rising.

It is the quiet road from Clones to Scarva, however, that

bears the legend of the mysterious man with the light, and regular reports of his appearance have kept this ghost story alive for many years.

Many local people avoid the road at night and subscribe emphatically to its reputation of being haunted. Some have described the apparition vaguely, merely as a large shadow seen between some bushes at a bend, while others have been more detailed in their descriptions, stating that they distinctly saw a tall, gaunt man dressed in a long cloak and carrying a light under his left arm.

The detail of the light, and the fact that it was under the left arm, seems to be a common factor in many local accounts of the apparition, which is also on record as having been seen clearly by one member of a party while remaining invisible to another.

One of the most convincing accounts of this Co. Monaghan ghost concerns one of the itinerant families with whom the road to Scarva was popular. One night, when the father and mother were away from the camp, a tall man in a long black coat entered the camp and seated himself with the children. So upset were the parents when they learned of this on their return that they shifted camp the next day and moved on to another district, an unexpected reaction surely from people accustomed to darkness and lonely places and, one would have thought, more inured to terrors of the night, real or supernatural, than the house-dweller.

In one form or another, evidence of the ghost of the Scarva road has turned up repeatedly over the years, either in reports of actual clear sightings, or vague shadows not easily accounted for, or in people claiming to have encountered the dreaded man in the cloak appearing at lonely houses at night, terrified by what they had seen and seeking shelter.

As in most cases of supernatural manifestations, the story of the cloaked man, while no firm explanation can be put forward, is sometimes linked locally with a happening from the past.

In the early part of the century, at the very spot where the apparition is most frequently seen, a man is said to have been beaten to death.

The Horses of Longfield

A ghost story that bears a thread of similarity with the legend of the foxes of Gormanston, in so far as it concerns an animal manifestation at time of death, is attached to an old County Tipperary mansion and a poor Italian boy who later made a valuable contribution to nineteenth century Ireland, where he settled down and became a wealthy and respected member of the community.

On a day in 1875, in an upper bedroom of secluded Longfield House, on the banks of the Suir, five miles north of Cashel, Charles Bianconi, once a penniless boy trying to sell cheap religious pictures around the scattered farmhouses of the Irish countryside, lay dying. Suddenly those present at his bedside heard the sound of galloping horses on the gravel driveway beneath his window. The clatter of hoof-beats continued, alternately fading away and then getting louder again.

When Bianconi's family and servants investigated, there were no horses near the house. The gates leading into the yard were closed, and none of the family's horses had broken loose.

Just as the foxes had emerged from their coverts to keep vigil in the closing moments of the lives of the Viscounts Gormanston, it was singularly fitting that Bianconi's death should be associated with the horse, the animal he had loved and employed so usefully in Ireland.

Charles Bianconi arrived from Italy in 1802, when he was sixteen, and four years later opened his own shop, working as a carver and gilder. From his early travels around the countryside he realised that Ireland badly needed some form of public transport, and with the idea of filling this need, began to save money. When he had sufficient, he bought a humble 'side car', drawn by one horse and capable only of carrying four passengers. It made the first journey of a regular service between Clonmel and Cahir on 5 July 1815.

The venture was a success, and presently other towns were linked, Limerick and Thurles being the first. Bianconi's cars, or 'the Bians', as they came to be called, soon spread in a network all over the country. To cope with increasing demand, larger vehicles were built, culminating in the huge 'Finn

An early form of transport on the roads of Ireland, introduced by a far-seeing young Italian named Charles Bianconi. . . to whom phantom horses paid homage as he lay dying in Longfield House, near Cashel, Co. Tipperary, in 1875.

McCools'. By 1825 they were covering one thousand miles per day.

An important factor in Bianconi's spectacular success was the attention and care he gave to his horses. Most of these were animals which had been specially bred for the army, and were no longer needed because of the ending of the Napoleonic wars. He always saw to it that they were well fed and well groomed, and at one time owned no fewer than nine hundred horses. The strange manifestation at the hour of his death is, therefore, all the more acceptable.

Charles Bianconi is buried beside the Catholic church at Boherlahan, near his old home, where a Romanesque chapel marks his family vault.

Stranger at Castletown

The ghost of a gentleman in a long grey coat, walking down a staircase ten years before that staircase was built; a mysterious guest who left behind him a grim and permanent souvenir of his visit. These are two of the weird legends of the house known as Castletown, in Celbridge, Co Kildare.

It is fitting, indeed, that Ireland's best known, and certainly most magnificent, stately home should have a ghost or two of its own. Built by William Connolly, Speaker of the Irish House of Commons, and always referred to as 'Speaker Connolly', Castletown was the finest achievement of a man who devoted much of his time to erecting residences for himself.

The strange visitor to Castletown came in 1767, when the then owner of the mansion, Thomas Connolly, a grand nephew of the Speaker, had spent the day hunting with the local pack. Returning home alone in the dusk, he was joined by another rider, whom, he assumed, had also been following the hunt, although he could not remember having seen him before.

Connolly, always a ready and hospitable host, invited the stranger back to Castletown, where, he knew, his usual group of friends would be gathered to round off the day's sport. The stranger accepted the invitation and the two men rode on to the mansion.

Later in the evening, having availed of Connolly's liberal hospitality, the stranger fell asleep in his chair. Thinking that his unknown guest might be more comfortable if his heavy riding bots were removed, Connolly instructed a servant to do this. To the horror of the other guests and their host, when the manservant pulled off the stranger's boots a cloven foot was revealed.

At that moment, the stranger awoke, jumped to his feet and faced the other occupants of the big dining room defiantly, mocking them with screams and diabolical laughter. When a priest who was present threw a missal at him, the book passed through him and smashed against the large mirror over the fireplace, breaking it into a hundred fragments. Still screaming at them, the stranger was suddenly surrounded by a burst of vivid yellow flame, and when this vanished, the stranger, too, had disappeared.

When they had recovered their composure, Connolly and his terrified guests found that, at the spot where their visitor had stood at the fireplace, the huge hearthstone bore a deep crack. The crack survives to the present day.

The second occurrence, that of the man in the long grey coat, was first experienced by Speaker Connolly's widow who survived her husband by many years. The lady's first sight of this apparition was on the top gallery. She heard mocking laughter, and saw the figure moving, following the descent of the grand staircase, which at that time had not been built. When it was added, ten years later, it corresponded exactly to the apparition's movements.

It is, perhaps, mere coincidence that this legend of demoniac manifestation is attached to a house built by a man who was also the owner of the Hell Fire Club at Montpellier in the Dublin mountains, a building which has its own grim record of entertaining the devil.

Speaker Connolly's proud mansion in Co. Kildare was bought from Lord Carew by the Honourable Desmond Guinness in 1965, and restored superbly to its original glory, becoming the headquarters of the Irish Georgian Society, and an active and superlative centre for numerous cultural activities.

The novelist Nancy Mitford, an aunt of Desmond Guinness, attended the sale in 1965 and afterwards wrote: 'Castletown fetched the price of a nice Paris flat – with about 500 acres of land thrown in and several old masters which some enthusiastic ancestress of Lord Carew had stuck to the walls!'

The house is open to the public, and the cracked hearthstone, grim souvenir of the events related, may still be seen.

And. . . who knows?. . . today, when an audience is gathered in the grand gallery at Castletown at dusk, faintly, through the sounds of a sonata, an alert ear may hear the faint echo of mocking laughter from the past.

The Dargle Lovers

Every Midsummer Eve, the ghost of a beautiful girl is said to appear in a Co. Wicklow glen, eternally seeking the young lover she betrayed.

This romantic legend is one of many attached to the Dargle valley, near Bray, and is centred around the massive rock that juts over the glen, known as the Lovers' Leap.

A young lady of the locality was faithless to her lover, giving her attentions, instead, to another young man, who had started to woo her with dash and charm. But while she was singing a favourite song to please him, as she paused between verses, she heard the distant toll of a church bell, unmistakably signifying a death. On inquiring, and with a terrible fear clutching her heart, she discovered that her former lover, stricken by her unfaithfulness, had died of a broken heart.

Overcome by remorse, she left her new admirer and hurried to the graveyard where they had just buried the youth who had died. There, despite the entreaties of her friends, she spent a night of sleet and rain at his graveside. On each following night she came again, and although her worried family tried to dissuade her, she continued her lonely vigil, only going back to her home during daylight hours.

Indifferent to the pleadings of those who loved her, and the entreaties of her new admirer, who had been responsible for her desertion of the dead youth, she continued to spend each night at the graveside, determined, it seemed, to die for him who had died for her.

In the haunted Dargle valley in Co. Wicklow. . . the centre of the village of Enniskerry, as it was in the late 1920s, looking towards the Powerscourt demesne. Close by is the Dargle River's Lovers' Leap, with its echoes of an old romance ending in tragedy, remembered in the Midsummer Eve legend of the ghost of a lovely girl in the shape of a dove or a white fawn, forever seeking her lost lover through the quiet woodlands.

Eventually, inevitably, her mind collapsed, and she told her distraught sister that her lover had risen from the grave and walked with her through the Dargle glen, promising to meet her again and take her to a place where they would be together forever.

Much alarmed, the girl's family tried to keep her confined to the house, but she managed to escape. Her absence was discovered a few minutes later, and her brother quickly followed her, heading with all speed to the churchyard, where he knew he would find her.

He arrived too late, only in time to catch a glimpse of her scarf fluttering in the breeze as she ran towards the river. Trying desperately to overtake her, he saw her climb up the huge crag surmounting the Dargle, pause a moment on its treacherous brink and then plunge into the swollen river below, doubtless lured to her death by the phantom lover conjured up by her tortured imagination.

This is the romantic tragedy that is one of the legends of this Wicklow beauty spot. It claims that the spirit of the unhappy girl, each year on Midsummer Eve, revisits the headland above the river, sometimes in the form of a dove, 'floating like a silver star through the night', sometimes in the shape of a white fawn, dashing forward and disappearing into the shadows of the woods.

The Phantom Coach of Newlands

In the still of the night, a phantom coach is said to career along a narrow, curving driveway, swaying and creaking in its urgency, towards Newlands House. . . in a grisly re-enactment of a long-ago day of rebellion, violence and murder.

The Georgian mansion is today the clubhouse of Newlands Golf Club, at Clondalkin, Co. Dublin, but time was when it was a proud private residence, that, in its day, knew a succession of distinguished owners and an equally impressive range of famous visitors.

Newlands House is little changed since its days of glory. Although in recent years alterations have been made to the main entrance, and a modern bar built at the rear of the building, most of the original features of the house have been preserved, notably in the massive drawing room, a spacious apartment that must have compared favourably with the best of its era, with its huge windows and magnificent ceiling. Its priceless Bozzi fireplace still survives, surmounted by a large gilt-framed painting of a half-naked woman, a mute relic of the mansion's heyday as a private residence.

Undoubtedly the best-known owner of Newlands House was Mr Arthur Wolfe, later Baron Kilwarden and Chief Justice of Ireland. . . whose ghostly coach still speeds, it is said, on dark nights, back to the house from which it carried him on the day of his death.

Kilwarden had attained high office through the patronage of the Earl of Tyrone and the influence of the Beresfords rather than through any particular talent of his own. On first acquaintance he appeared taciturn, but had a mercurial knack of changing to almost boyish joviality. At the bar, he was a colleague and friend of the much younger Jonah Barrington, who tells us that 'like certain humorous characters on the stage, he frequently worked himself into silly anger by endeavouring to show that he was perfectly good-tempered.'

If Kilwarden was not always lucky in his relations with those who did not know him well, he was tragically unfortunate on that day in 1803 when Robert Emmet's insurrection broke out in Dublin.

At home in Newlands with his family, Kilwarden received a Government summons to the city, and, without knowing of the rebellion, set off from Clondalkin in his coach, accompanied by one of his daughters and his nephew, a clergyman. By ill luck his coachman drove straight into the thick of the rebellion and the coach was attacked. Barrington claimed that the crowd confused Kilwarden with Lord Carleton, who, a few years before, as Justice of the Common Pleas, had tried and condemned the two Sheers brothers.

The attackers allowed the girl to escape, but killed the clergyman, and than launched themselves on Kilwarden. The murder is recalled in the vivid contemporary words of Barrington:

Hundreds of the murderers now surrounded the carriage,

ambitious only who should first spill the blood of the chief-justice; a multitude of pikemen at once assailed him, but his wounds proved that he had made many efforts to evade them. His hands were lacerated all over in the act of resistance; but after a long interval of torture, near thiry stabs in various parts of his body incapacitated him from struggling further with his destiny. They dragged him into the street; yet, when conveyed into a house, he was still sensible, and able to speak a few words, but soon after expired, to the great grief of all those who knew him well, as I did, and were able to separate his frivolity from his excellent qualities.

Some old golfing enthusiasts, playing the game since the 1920s, when Newlands was known as the Robin Hood Club, recall hearing of Kilwarden's phantom coach, in days when the eerie story, told in the clubhouse on winter nights, was given considerable atmosphere by the very isolation of the old mansion, and when the walk home afterwards down the long drive to the main gates, along which the ghostly coach was said to career, was a dismal, even terrifying prospect at the close of an evening's conviviality.

And, today, when the evening conversation of golfers has faded, and the lights have been extinguished in the gracious apartment that was once Lord Kilwarden's drawing room, perhaps the silent lady in the gilt frame above the Bozzi fireplace smiles down on other figures in this room that has witnessed so many changing times and so many diverse personalities.

The Tallaght Ghost

Many is the lonely road of Ireland accredited by local superstition with being the setting for the appearance of the dreaded 'headless coach', an apparition recorded almost as frequently as the banshee, and, like the fairy woman, looked upon as a warning of death to the beholder.

The coach was said to career madly through the countryside at dead of night, driven by a headless coachman and drawn by headless horses; a Dracula-like entourage, that could well have been imported from the folklore of Transylvania.

Oldbawn, Tallaght, the seventeenth century mansion of Archdeacon Bulkeley, shortly before it was demolished in the present century. After his death, the Archdeacon's phantom coach with headless horses and a headless coachman, became a chilling legend of the district.

There were few areas of Ireland in which fireside accounts of the headless coach were not common, and it was a regular stand-by of neighbourhood story-tellers in counties rich in tradition, like Wexford and Wicklow. Indeed, even in Co. Dublin itself, there were reports of three miniature hearses having been seen on a road close to the scene of a mass murder in the 1920s, while a road at Donabate has long been known locally as 'the hearse road'.

In south Co. Dublin there is also a headless coach story. Tallaght, like Cabra on the north side of the city, is today a teeming new suburb, already a far cry from the lonely rural district it was until the 1950s.

The phantom coach of Tallaght, with a headless coachman, drawn by six headless horses and containing a ghostly passenger, was said to career regularly along the lonely roads in the foothills of the Dublin mountains, and for many years it struck terror into the hearts of people living in the area.

The phantom occupant of the coach was thought to be Archdeacon Bulkeley, who, in the seventeenth century, lived in a fine old mansion at Tallaght, called Oldbawn House.

Bulkeley was an extensive landowner in the district, and many legends centred around Oldbawn in his lifetime and after his death, but none of these was more chilling than the strangely persistent tradition of his ghostly nocturnal journeys.

A more realistic reminder of the archdeacon survives today in the National Museum in Kildare Street, Dublin, where a great fireplace and a staircase from Oldbawn House are preserved.

The Leering Face

Among the most frightening apparitions ever seen must surely be that encountered one night in the spring of 1966 by a young couple driving along a lonely country road in County Louth.

Margaret Johnston, who was 21 at the time and living with her family on the outskirts of the village of Termonfeckin, not far from Drogheda, was driving with her boyfriend near her home, and was passing by the estate of a retired British Army colonel, when they both saw the spectre, 'a huge horse with a man's face and horrible bulging eyes'.

Miss Johnston was in a severe state of shock after the encounter, and in an interview with a Dublin newspaper some time later stated: 'It was terrible. I can't forget it and I haven't eaten for days since the night it happened.'

In her own words, Margaret gave a graphic account of the incident at the time.

'I was with John Farrell from Milltown House, Corntown, Kells. It was after midnight and we were driving in his car past Lord Dillon's place. Suddenly, John was forced to break hard as a horse loomed up before us. I was thrown back on the seat. When I looked out the window I saw this monster or ghost or whatever it was.

'I could see by John's face that he saw it too. I think I screamed, but both of us were so frightened that we were paralysed. The thing had a horse's body. But it was the face, leering and hairy and huge which shocked.

'The animal stretched right across the road and completely blocked the car. It stayed there for nearly two minutes. We were petrified. Then it vanished. John quickly swung the car around and drove to my home, about a mile away.

'We were so frightened that we drove through the gate and knocked it off the hinges. I woke up my father and both of us told him the same story. We don't drink and two of us couldn't have imagined the same thing.'

This was borne out by the girl's father, Mr John Johnston, when the story was followed up by the *Sunday Press*. Mr Johnston, a lorry driver, told a reporter: 'They must have seen something awful. Both were still terrified when they came in here and each of their descriptions of the ghost tallied. Margaret was very sick for days after the incident.'

An interesting sidelight on the affair was given by Lord Dillon, the owner of Rath House, outside which the couple saw the apparition. In the course of an interview a short while later, he said:

'I have just returned from London today, but my man told me that some local girl had seen something or other. We have a white pony here and perhaps it was this. I don't know. I know the Johnston girl. She used to work here and she's most respectable and reliable.'

A story known in the district concerns a hoof print embedded in the stone steps in front of Rath House, and when reminded of this, Lord Dillon said:

> Well, tradition has it that in the eighteenth century the then owner of the place, a Protestant, had aroused the wrath of the parish priest.
>
> It is said that the priest rode up on his horse one day to discuss some matter or other, but the landlord ordered him off the lands. The landlord stood on the steps of the house and used violent threats to the priest and his parish-ioners.
>
> The story goes that the priest's horse suddenly reared and crashed his hoof on the step. There is what appears to be a hoofprint on the steps today.
>
> We came to live in the house only about eleven years ago, so I'm only going on what I've heard. I suppose it's an interesting link with the recent happening.

Whatever it was that Margaret Johnston and John Farrell saw on that frightening night in 1966, and whatever may be the explanation for the apparition, Termonfeckin is an historic place. It grew up around a sixth century monastic settlement of St Fechin, had a convent, approved by Celestine III, in 1195, and at different times was a place of residence for both the Catholic and Protestant Archbishops of Armagh. There is a tenth century richly ornamented cross in the local graveyard, and, on a hill to the east of the village, stands a fifteenth century castle.

A place with many links with the past; a place too, perhaps, of unquiet spirits.

The Footsteps of Foulksrath

The sound of footsteps suddenly breaking the silence of the night, followed almost immediately by the creaking noise of a door being opened and then slowly being closed again is one of the legends of sixteenth century Foulksrath Castle. This sturdy, castellated building with its high, commanding main tower, is eight miles from Kilkenny city on the road to the village of Ballyragget. This is where the Great Countess of Ormonde once lived and from where she rode out on forays at the head of her own troops.

There is no explanation for the ghostly noises that echo through the ancient top floor of Foulksrath each year on one particular night in early November, but the castle is situated in a lonely stretch of Ormonde country. 'Black Thomas' Ormonde himself, Lieutenant-General of Queen Elizabeth's forces in Ireland, was captured in a spectacular move by Owen MacRory O'More in Ballyragget in 1600, and in Saint Kieran Street, in nearby Kilkenny City, Kyteler's Inn is redolent of the activities of Dame Alice Kyteler, who, in 1324 was accused of witchcraft, and of poisoning her four husbands.

Foulksrath Castle was built early in the sixteenth century by the family of Hugh Purcell, who acted as Strongbow's first lieutenant, and is himself associated with another legend attached to the old building.

There is, within the great bulk of the castle, one particular small room with a romantic folklore of its own. Any girl who spends the night in it, and who hears the cuckoo when she awakens the following morning, will shortly find her true lover and will be married within the year.

The story behind this legend is that Hugh Purcell had an attractive daughter, who met and fell in love with a local man named O'Brennan. He wished to marry her, but the young man antagonised the girl's father, and Purcell, in the forthright fashion of some fathers of the time, in what seemed to promise to be an effective means of preventing the marriage, had his daughter placed forcibly in the small, well-guarded room in the castle.

Soon, however, help came in the form of a bird, a cuckoo, which was used by the young lovers to establish a line of communication between themselves, although how this link was achieved, whether by using the bird as a carrier of notes, or through the intervention of some supernatural agency that bestowed unusual powers on it, is not clear. Whatever the explanation, the legend has a happy ending, for the bird's appearance and its subsequent use by the couple helped the young man to plan the rescue of Purcell's daughter, whom he later married.

For many years, Foulksrath Castle remained unused and

neglected, but in the 1940s it was purchased by the Irish youth organisation, An Oige, and, just as they had done at Aughavannagh, the former British blockhouse in Co. Wicklow with its ghost of the hangman Hempenstall, members of the group repaired and restored it, transforming the old pile into a well-serviced hostel for young hikers.

In 1976, Mrs Paula Dunne, from Rathfarnham, Co. Dublin, who, with her husband Brian, was appointed warden of the hostel, was reminded by the *Evening Press* of the old stories centred about her home, and asked if she had ever heard the ghostly footsteps on the castle's top floor and the sounds of the door opening and closing.

'We have been here two years,' she replied, 'and have not heard the ghost yet.' Then she added: 'I would not be here now if we had.'

But Foulksrath's eerie reputation endures, and perhaps adds to its appeal for the many hundreds of holidaymakers who visit it each year. . . especially if, by chance, they arrive on a certain night in early November when the upper floor of the old keep is not as silent as it might be.

A Warning at Boley

The apparition of a little old woman with a limp, issuing the warning, 'You are not to sleep here tonight', in an old Victorian mansion near Dun Laoghaire, has been recounted for me by the well known Dublin columnist Terry O'Sullivan and underlined convincingly by his own personal experiences in the house.

Rory O'Connor Park, Kill O' The Grange, Dun Laoghaire, Co. Dublin, is now the site of a small colony of attractive modern houses, built on the grounds of an undistinguished mansion named Boley, home of the late Sir Valentine Grace, who once acted with the Abbey company, playing the lead in a play called *General John Regan*.

Sir Valentine's Victorian mansion, in Terry O'Sullivan's own words,

was strictly upstairs and downstairs, and even sideways. I

rented the wing which meant that the billiard room (without a table) was my drawing, living, reception and general purposes room. It looked unfurnished with two chairs and a sack of coal. There was no covering on the floorboards. There was a eucalyptus tree outside.

I mentioned to the awesome figure of the late Professor J. B. Whelehan that I was going to live in Boley. He then lived in a minor Edwardian mansion called 'Stradbrook', now, I think, a convent.

He advised me not to go to live in Boley. The tenants of his lodge had gone to live in precisely where I proposed to live. . . the right wing. . . and they had left the next day. During the night their furniture had been disturbed, and they had heard inexplicable noises. 'Rubbish,' I thought, and moved in. Nothing happened. . . till one bitter winter night.

The night was foul, and I had a guest who had no car and no commitments about getting home. So I made up a roaring fire and a snug cot bed in front of the fire and said goodnight. He woke me up half an hour later and said: 'There is something funny going on here. There is someone knocking on the door, like this' (and he rapped on the table. . . three times and then twice), 'but when I open the door there is nobody there.'

So I sat up with the craggy Kerryman till sleep, the most powerful drug, ended the irrational vigil.

There came to visit me another night, a warm friend from Tipperary, one George Ryan. He stroked a UCD four (and, indeed, I had been cox for a while), and I mention this to make it clear that the next subject was no neurotic, but a strong, fit and healthy man. . . who, of course, had no inkling of Professor Whelehan's advice to me not to live there, and who knew nothing of the knocking on the door.

Another dirty night. No car. I stacked up the huge fire, made up a snug bed, said goodnight to George Ryan, and went up to the bathroom to wash my teeth.

A knock on the door. There was my guest, who said: 'I can't sleep here tonight. I was just pulling up the bedclothes when I distinctly heard a voice say, "You are not to sleep here tonight".'

I sat up all night with the big man from Thurles.

But so far nothing had happened to me; enough to make me curious, but not frightened. So I went down to have a chat with the then Parish Priest of Monkstown. . . and I told him what I have told you.

'Ah yes,' he said, 'we have been asked on several occasions to visit where you live and to bless the place. There is some soul in trouble there.'

But still nothing happened to me.

So I went up to the blacksmith in the forge of Kill O' The Grange. He was shoeing a horse, and I asked him if he had ever heard any strange things about Boley, the home of Sir Valentine Grace, and without raising his head from the labour of driving the nails into the shoe resting in the crook of his elbow, he said 'Of course. We all know your place is haunted. It is haunted by Lady Grace. The ghost is dressed in black and wears a bonnet, and walks with a limp. She has been seen there quite often.'

I went back to the collection of outhouses and cottages, converted from stables, and there the senior citizens told me with indifference that of course the place I lived in was haunted by a little lady with a limp.

Years after I told Sir Raymond Grace, a journalist with the *Irish Times*, all these bits of a jigsaw puzzle at a lunch in the Shelbourne, and he listened intently and said: 'You have described my grandmother.' The little lady in black with the bonnet walked with a limp because she was one of the fashionable ladies contemporary with Queen Alexandra, wife of King Edward VII. Alexandra walked with a limp. Therefore, the ladies invited to the soirees in Dublin Castle in the early years of this century affected a limp.

But the little dark lady never appeared to me.

Boley, lands and houses, are built over now, but one curious link remains with the little lady in black – the stump of a tree.

Outside Boley, its elephant grey Victorian hide beginning to flake, there was a magnificent eucalyptus tree. That tree dominated the fields and gardens around, and had no rival. Under it by day babies slept in prams, and by night the dark lady knocked on my door and spoke. . . 'You are not to sleep here tonight.'

I do not know why, but the stump of the forty foot high eucalyptus tree has been preserved on the village green of Rory O'Connor Park, and the stump, like a neglected totem pole, is there without rhyme or reason.

The forge in Kill O' The Grange is there too, a snug home, now occupied by Liam Larkin and his family. And Mrs Raymond Grace breeds boxer dogs.

So, in a way, everybody is accounted for, except the little ghost with the bonnet and the limp.

Has she no home to go to?

That we have not yet heard the last of the hauntings at Boley is suggested by more recent events that took place in May 1977.

The surviving stump of the eucalyptus tree referred to by Terry O'Sullivan, the last reminder of the old Grace Mansion, was removed early in May, to facilitate the parking of cars, but within a matter of weeks strange happenings began to occur in Rory O'Connor Park.

Several residents heard singing in the still of the night, usually starting around one o'clock. At first, it was thought to be the work of a practical joker, or a home-going drunk, but these possibilities were quickly ruled out, as more local people heard the weird sound and failed to trace its source, although several claimed that what they heard faintly resembled the opening lines of 'Old Man River' or 'Danny Boy'.

Five schoolboys, camping in a garden, heard the singing and were frightened indoors. As the phenomenon continued unexplained, the old legend of Boley was remembered. A youth, 18-year-old Jimmy Meegan, managed to take a tape recording of the sounds. In this, a wailing voice calls for help, and then breaks into 'Old Man River'.

Mrs Maire Fitzgibbon, whose home overlooks the site of the eucalyptus tree, has lived in the area since childhood, and remembers seeing Sir Valentine Grace, who had the reputation of being a good singer. She maintains that the estate was sold on condition that its trees would not be felled.

The Headless Rider

In Dublin for many years one of the best known ghost stories of the north city was that of a fearsome headless rider on a white horse, said to be seen occasionally in the dead of night on Jones's Road, a thoroughfare very familiar to all supporters of Gaelic football and hurling, as it contains the main entrance to Croke Park.

This apparition was said to be the ghost of the man who gave his name to this Dublin Street, a one-time City Sheriff and gambler named Buck Jones, who lived on nearby Clonliffe Road, in a mansion later incorporated in the grounds of Holy Cross College and known today as The Red House.

The street today bears Jones's name, for it began as a pathway cut by him, from the North Circular Road to Clonliffe Road, to give him easy access to his house and spare him the alternative roundabout journey by way of Drumcondra Road. His pathway also embraced the present Russell Street.

There is little on record about Buck Jones's official activities while he was City Sheriff, and he would appear, indeed, to have been more enthusiastic in pandering to his great weakness for gambling that he was to executing his professional duties.

On one occasion, however, Jones showed his mettle, when a band of brigands broke into his home to steal his silverware. He promptly attacked the intruders with a brace of pistols and the foray that followed resulted in the deaths of two of the raiders.

This dramatic encounter of Jones's was not perhaps surprising, as his house stood close to the notorious Mud Island at Ballybough, for long the haunt of highwaymen and footpads, who, at that time, were a constant threat to travellers from the city foolhardy enough to pass through the area.

And, indeed, City Sheriff though he was, Jones himself was to fall foul of the law when his persistent gambling led to his downfall and he found himself thrown into the Marshalsea Barracks, which had been built close to the quays in the 1740s as a debtor's prison and which, for a time, also served as an arsenal for Robert Emmet and his followers.

Jones died in prison and is buried in Ballybough, at the end of Clonliffe Road, not far from his once proud mansion, at a spot close to where an old graveyard and a gibbet were once located.

If Buck Jones's ghost rides through this haunted area he knew so well, other ghosts must join him for it is a district rich in history, and even before pirates roamed Mud Island, it was the probable site of the climax of the Battle of Clontarf.

In 1895, James Joyce was living in 17 North Richmond Street, close to the O'Connell Schools, which Edmund Rice had founded, and where Joyce himself attended for about a year, while forty years earlier Matt Talbot was born in Aldborough Court.

The 1916 leader Sean McDermott lived at 16 Russell Place, and at that end of Jones's Road now called Russell Street lived Brendan Behan and his uncle Peadar Kearney, who wrote the words to Patrick Heeney's music for the Irish national anthem, 'The Soldier's Song'.

And yet another house in the immediate area of Jones's Road, 27 Upper Rutland Street, was once the home of a future President of Ireland, Sean T. O'Ceallaigh, and it was there that he sheltered the brothers Padraic and Willie Pearse, when their own home was considered too dangerous, on the eve of the 1916 Rising.

A place of ghosts, surely, a haunted setting, on some dark night, for a headless rider on a white horse.

HOW OFT HAS THE BANSHEE CRIED

How oft has the Banshee cried!
How oft has death untied
    Bright links that Glory wove,
    Sweet bonds entwined by Love!
Peace to each manly soul that sleepeth;
Rest to each faithful eye that weepeth;
    Long may the fair and the brave
Sigh o'er the hero's grave!

    We're fallen upon gloomy days!
    Star after star decays,
    Every bright name that shed
    Light o'er the land is fled.

Close to the haunted castle of Skryne, historic Tara, Ireland's most storied hill, ancient seat of the High Kings, with its ghosts of Cuchulain and Queen Maeve, cursed by St 'Ruadhan of Lorrha, who, to avenge a wrong done to his nephew Guaire by King Dermot, assembled his priests and to the chanting of psalms and the tolling of bells cursed the wooden palaces of Tara. Today, the former glory of throne room and banquet hall has departed and only the outline of old earthworks remains.

The Georgian mansion on Clonliffe Road in Dublin that was the home of Buck Jones, as it looked in the 1890s. Jones was a City Sheriff, fated to be thrown into a debtor's prison, from which he was released only shortly before his death. He was buried close to his old home, at Ballybough, and his ghost, in the form of a headless horseman, terrorised the district for decades. The house survives today, and is in use as the Dublin Diocesan Press Office.

Dark falls the tear of him who mourneth
Lost joy, or hope that ne'er returneth:
  But brightly flows the tear
Wept o'er a hero's bier.

  Quench'd are our beacon lights –
Thou, of the Hundred Fights!
Thou, on whose burning tongue
Truth, peace, and freedom hung!
Both mute, – but long as valour shineth,
Or mercy's soul at war repineth,
  So long shall Erin's pride
Tell how they lived and died.

Thomas Moore

Farmyard Phantom

In all records of paranormal experiences numerous examples are to be found in which appearances of ghosts coincide with deaths, as in the case of the Clongowes story. One of the most bizarre of these comes from Co. Tyrone, from the remote townland of Cavankirk in the Clogher Valley.

Details of the Cavankirk apparition come from an old magazine file, but, as it happened as recently as the 1890s, must still be remembered in the Clogher Valley.

Here, on a lonely farm, a family named Wilson lived, consisting of the mother and father, two brothers and a sister. After their parents's deaths, the children continued to live in the house. Soon, however, one of the boys became wayward and was a constant source of worry to the other two, especially his sister, who did her best to reform him.

Despite all her efforts, however, things went from bad to worse, and the more she scolded him the more her brother defied his sister, landing himself in one scrape after another. Eventually, wishing to escape the restrictions of home, the boy emigrated to Canada.

One evening George, the brother who remained at home on the farm, brought the cows in from the fields and put them in the byre as usual to be milked. He went into the house for his tea, while his sister at once left the house, bringing with her the pails for milking.

As he was seated at the table, George thought he saw, from the corner of his eye, a shadow flit past the window. A moment later he heard his sister screaming.

Rushing outside, George found his sister lying on the ground in the byre, in a state of terror and collapse. It was some time before he had calmed her sufficiently for her to tell him what had happened.

The girl told him a frightening story. She had looked up from her milking to see her younger brother enter the byre, and thought at first that he had returned unexpectedly from Canada. But then, to her consternation, he had thrown himself at her and attempted to throttle her. Only the sudden entry of George had stopped the attack. Her assailant, as he turned, had looked back at her malevolently, and she knew, at that moment, that the face was indeed that of her younger brother, but that he was not in the byre in flesh and blood. Afterwards, other disturbances occurred at the Wilson home. These usually took the form of loud noises at night in the kitchen, when nobody was present in the room.

Neighbours and friends were called in by the brother and sister, but even when several people were under the roof, the trouble continued, usually centred in the kitchen, and resembling the sound of articles of furniture being hurled from one end of the room to the other. On one occasion, when the sister had retired to her own room to rest on the bed, she was viciously attacked, unseen hands attempting to strangle her.

Shortly afterwards, the Wilsons received a letter from Canada. It informed them that the younger boy had died. His death had occurred on the day of the first attack on his sister in the byre.

Unable to endure their old home any longer, George Wilson sold the farm and emigrated to America.

The Radiant Boy

As Henry James has illustrated so chillingly in *The Turn of the Screw*, there is something particularly sinister in the association of children with the supernatural, even when there is an absence of that evil which was such an important feature of the only play which James wrote and which was transcribed by Jack Clayton in the film version, *The Innocents*.

Child ghosts have been common enough, and manifestations like that of the boy in the gatelodge of Rathfarnham Castle and the little girl in Dublin's Shelbourne Hotel, recorded by Hans Holzer, and covered in other chapters of this book, assert themselves from time to time, to remind us that, whatever other barriers limit the spirit world, age is not one of them.

In the last century, apparitions of boys appeared in several haunted houses, and each of these was referred to as a 'radiant boy'. A well-known German authority of the time, Dr Kerner, claimed that one such apparition appeared only once in every seven years and was connected with the murder of a child by its mother. Another, thought to concern Corby Castle in Cumberland, was quoted by the nineteenth century writer, Mrs Crowe, in her *Night Side of Nature*, and owes its source to a manuscript written in the castle in December 1824.

The ghost of a 'radiant boy' in the North of Ireland, although the exact location of the apparition is not given, is recorded in John H. Ingram's *The Haunted Homes and Family Legends of Great Britain*, with acknowledgements to the prolific Mrs Crowe. Ingram's book was published by Messrs W. H. Allen in the early 1880s, but the story itself dates from the end of the eighteenth century.

Ingram thought that, although several other writers had recorded it, Mrs Crow's version, in her *Ghost Stories*, was 'less romantically told than usual, and, consequently, has a greater air of *vraisemblance*'. Mrs Crowe obtained the story in this form from the family of Lord Castlereagh, who had seen the ghost of the boy:

> Captain Stewart, afterwards Lord Castlereagh, when he was a young man, happened to be quartered in Ireland. He was fond of sport, and one day the pursuit of game carried him

so far that he lost his way.

The weather, too, had become very rough, and in this strait he presented himself at the door of a gentleman's house, and, sending in his card, requested shelter for the night. The hospitality of the Irish country gentry is proverbial; the master of the house received him warmly, said he feared he could not make his so comfortable as he could have wished, his house being full of visitors already.

Added to which, some strangers, driven by the inclemency of the night, had sought shelter before him; but that such accommodation as he could give he was heartily welcome to: whereupon he called his butler, and, committing his guest to his good offices, told him he must put him up somewhere, and do the best he could for him. There was no lady, the gentleman being a widower.

Captain Stewart found the house crammed, and a very jolly party it was. His host invited him to stay, and promised him good shooting if he would prolong his visit a few days; and, in fine, he thought himself extremely fortunate to have fallen into such pleasant quarters.

At length, after an agreeable evening, they all retired to bed, and the butler conducted him to a large room almost divested of furniture, but with a blazing peat fire in the grate, and a shake-down on the floor, composed of cloaks and other heterogeneous materials. Nevertheless, to the tired limbs of Captain Stewart, who had had a hard day's shooting, it looked very inviting; but, before he lay down, he thought it advisable to take off some of the fire, which was blazing up the chimney in what he thought was an alarming manner. Having done this, he stretched himself upon the couch, and soon fell asleep.

He believed he had slept about a couple of hours when he awoke suddenly, and was startled by such a vivid light in the room that he thought it was on fire; but on turning to look at the grate he saw the fire was out, though it was from the chimney the light proceeded.

He sat up in bed, trying to discover what it was, when he perceived, gradually disclosing itself, the form of a beautiful naked boy, surrounded by a dazzling radiance. The boy looked at him earnestly, and then the vision faded, and all was dark.

Captain Stewart, so far from supposing what he had seen to be of a spiritual nature, had no doubt that the host, or the visitors, had been amusing themselves at his expense, and trying to frighten him. Accordingly, he felt indignant at the liberty; and, on the following morning, when he appeared at breakfast, he took care to evince his displeasure by the reserve of his demeanour, and by announcing his intention to depart immediately. The host expostulated, reminding him of his promise to stay and shoot. Captain Stewart coldly excused himself, and at length, the gentleman, seeing something was wrong, took him aside and pressed for an explanation; whereupon Captain Stewart, without entering into particulars, said that he had been made the victim of a sort of practical joking that he thought quite unwarrantable with a stranger.

The gentleman considered this not impossible amongst a parcel of thoughtless young men, and appealed to them to make an apology; but one and all, on their honour, denied the impeachment. Suddenly a thought seemed to strike him: he clapt his hand to his forehead, uttered an exclamation, and rang the bell.

'Hamilton,' said he to the butler, 'where did Captain Stewart sleep last night?'

'Well, Sir,' replied the man, in an apologetic tone, 'you know every place was full – the gentlemen were lying on the floor three or four in a room – so I gave him the *Boy's Room*; but I lit a blazing fire to keep him from coming out.'

'You were very wrong,' said the host; 'you know I have positively forbidden you to put anyone there, and have taken the furniture out of the room to insure its not being occupied.'

Then retiring with Captain Stewart, he informed him very gravely of the nature of the phenomenon he had seen; and at length, being pressed for further information, he confessed that there existed a tradition in his family that whomever the 'Radiant Boy' appeared to would rise to the summit of power, and when he reached the climax, would die a violent death; 'and I must say,' he added, 'the records that have been kept of his appearance go to confirm this persuasion.'

Ingram adds his own codicil: 'It is scarcely necessary to remind the reader that subsequently Lord Castlereagh became head of the Government, and, finally, perished by his own hand.'

Viscount Castlereagh was British Minister of War and Foreign Secretary during the Napoleonic wars and was extremely unpopular because of the bad condition of home affairs. He became Marquis of Londonderry in 1821 and committed suicide the following year, at the age of 53.

John H. Ingram, to whom I am indebted for the foregoing story was a prolific writer and editor of the 1880s. As well as *The Haunted Homes and Family Legends of Great Britain*, he edited, for Messrs W. H. Allen, London, a series of books on eminent women, including George Eliot, Emily Brontë, George Sand, Mary Lamb, Margaret Fuller, Maria Edgeworth and Elizabeth Fry. In a Preface to his own ghost book, he wrote:

> Particulars of the manner of the haunting is generally difficult to obtain: nearly every ancient castle, or time-worn hall, bears the reputation of being thus troubled, but in a very large majority of such cases no evidence is forthcoming – not even the ghost of a tradition! Guide-books, topographical works, even the loquacious custodian – where there is one – of the building, fail to furnish any details; were it otherwise, instead of one modest volume a many-tomed cyclopedia would be necessary.
>
> To mention here separately the many sources whence the information contained in this compilation has been drawn would be impossible, and as in most instances the authority has been specified under its respective heading, would be needless; but still thanks are due and are hereby tendered to those authors whose books have been made use of and to those noblemen and gentlemen who have aided the work by their friendly information.

Across a century, we re-echo Mr Ingram's words.

HELENA BLUNDEN, THE LINEN WORKER

Helena Cecilia Blunden was 16 when she began working in the spinning room of the linen mill. The eldest daughter of a Tyrone woman and a Kilkenny man, Helena had been born in Ireland but brought up in England.

In 1911, the Blundens returned to Ireland and settled in Belfast. An ardent Home Ruler, Helena's father would have preferred to settle in Dublin but Helena's uncles on her mother's side had already arranged jobs for the Blundens in Belfast.

Helena was a diligent, popular worker in the linen mill. A loud, cheerful, young woman, her head was full of the romanticism of Yeats' poetry, the wit of Shaw's plays and the raucous songs of the London music halls. Her grand uncle had been a wandering Irish dancing master in Kilkenny. Helena had inherited his talent for dance but she was more interested in singing than dancing. As a child, she had sung in a school choir in England. At school she had excelled in Latin and developed an interest in Italian culture, which included the operas of Puccini and Verdi. Since returning to Ireland she had danced at Feiseanna in Dublin. Her father encouraged her aspirations to the stage but Helena's mother frowned upon the notion. Helena had grown up among the immigrant Irish in London but invented a peculiar English accent which impressed her fellow workers. Her aspirations and songs, her accent and memories of London always guaranteed her a captivated audience and she enjoyed the attention.

The work in the spinning room was arduous and repetitive. On warm days in summer when the heat reached boiling point, children and women often fainted. The atmosphere was always damp with stale air, condensation settled on the walls and floors of the mill. Margaret Maxwell was a tough woman who in her youth had brawled with men and women in the street. No longer fit to fight or work in the flax room, Margaret was employed in the afternoons to mop and clean the condensation from the stairs. Pride made her resent the work but necessity made her stay. She was content to complain fiercely and scold anyone who dared to walk on the stairs while she mopped. She frightened the young children, but the adults only scorned her threats. She clashed often with Helena, deriding the young woman's songs and hope.

Helena worked 60 hours a week. On Saturday, the working day was supposed to finish at 12 noon but the workers always stayed late if an important order needed to be prepared. The linen company's first order had been to produce double damask linen tablecloths. These tablecloths were laid on the tables in the first class dining room on the Titanic.

The newly established company sometimes brought the workers in on Sundays to ensure orders were ready on time. On Sunday 14 April 1912, the workers including the half-timers in all departments came in to finish an order for Argentina. Helena was preoccupied with a concert she was due to attend in the parish hall that evening. She sang her way through the morning and into the afternoon and evening. At 2 pm, Helena realised that her work would not be complete by 6 pm and that there would be hardly any time between finishing in the mill and going to the concert. She kept her shoes on all day; ready to leave the minute her work was complete.

Margaret was tired before she even began her work on the stairs. She stooped over the mop and half-heartedly dabbled it along the top flight. She stopped to chastise a young half-timer who had only started and had not been warned about Margaret's stairs.

At 7 pm, Helena was finished. Already exhausted by excitement, heat and fasting, Helena went down the first flight. She tripped on the discarded mop, fell over the banister and down to the ground floor. Margaret heard the shrieking Helena and looked up to watch Helena falling. Margaret released her grip on the young boy and staggered down to the ground floor to discover that Helena was already dead.

Helena's intention had been to leave the linen mill forever and establish herself as a singer. Of course she may never have succeeded as a singer and may have been destined to stay in the spinning room for years, reminiscing about the times she had sung on stage. Her death at 16 dashed those aspirations. There are reasonable, sensible men and women today who say that Helena in death did not escape from the mill, that she still walks in that building.

The men and women who spent long hours in unhealthy working conditions to earn poor wages are today forgotten. Some of the mills still stand but the equipment has been removed and is now exhibited in museums for visitors to admire. Anonymous accounts of the memories and harsh experiences of mill workers are recorded. To imagine a mill worker's day, you should walk into an old mill, ascend the same stairs where hundreds of people walked, sit in a room where spinners once worked, ride in the screeching, heavy lift which was used to carry rolls of linen to the basement, look at the sturdy walls and wooden floors which were dampened by the workers' toil.

Built to house a linen mill in 1912, Flax House was occupied by linen manufacturers for over 50 years from 1912-1966. This five-storey, Edwardian building stands in the heart of the linen conservation area in Belfast city centre. With a shabby, forlorn appearance, the building is in an area or urban renewal which is now being rejuvenated with luxury loft apartments and modern offices. Two world wars, the sinking of the Titanic, the Easter Rising in 1916 and the evolution of modern Ireland have come and gone. With the decline of the linen industry, a series of short-term tenants and owners have moved in and out of the building. Vacant during periodic recessions in the 1980s and early 1990s, the printers has been in the building since 1991.

Paul McAvoy, Production Controller at the printers, is more concerned with booking cargo shipping and liaising with foreign customers than telling ghost stories. His week day begins at 8am and ends at 6pm. At weekends, he is often in from 10am until 2pm. He organises and supervises the dispatch of books from the basement and oversees the warehouse and printing press. At weekends and late in the evenings, Paul was often the only person in the building but more recently, he is reluctant to spend time alone in the building.

After only a few months moved into the building in 1991, Paul became aware of inexplicable noises: heavy thumps and movement of boxes, doors opening and no one entering, footsteps on the stairs and along the wooden corridors. Unfazed and sceptical, he initially interpreted the noises as the sounds of an old, creaking building.

Paul changed his mind only when someone unseen touched him. He described this physical encounter: "One Saturday morning I was in the warehouse running the press. I was worried that the press was going to trip so I was very occupied. I was expecting a colleague to arrive, I heard him come in and sensed him coming up beside me. I didn't take my eyes off the press to greet him but I knew he was there. I felt him tap me on the right shoulder four times and I looked around to greet him. There was no one beside me. When he eventually came in, I asked him if he had been in earlier but he said that he hadn't".

When Paul began to mention the strange sounds and eerie sensations, Tony and Charlie, his colleagues cajoled him with jibes about overwork and falling asleep at his desk. It was not long before they too noticed books and paper moved or hidden, with no one able to explain why the boxes had been moved.

Paul is certain that it is a woman who walks the floors of the building. He has heard her voice: "One day the three of us were down in the basement, and we all heard a woman's voice calling my name, 'Paul'. We looked around to see who was in but there was definitely no one there. Yet it was a voice within the basement, it wasn't someone outside".

On other occasions, a woman's voice calls out the name of one person in a group but only the individual hears her voice. Paul remembers many times when he worked alongside Tony and Charlie and heard someone calling his name. Each time Paul lifted his head from his work and looked up expecting to see someone coming up to him. Neither Tony nor Charlie who were beside him heard the voice, so Paul went back to work. It has not only happened to Paul. Charlie and Tony have each had the same experience.

Paul believes that there is an unseen inhabitant in the building: "Many's a time I get the sensation that there is someone else here. I remember there a few weeks ago, I heard Tony working in the light room. I called him a few times but I got no answer. I heard shuffling and the noise of someone moving around in the room, so I knew he was in there. A while later, Tony came up from downstairs and I said 'I called you, why didn't you answer?' But he said he'd been downstairs for the last 20 minutes. I said 'Well, there's been somebody in there moving around, I heard them'".

The web camera was first installed on Hallowe'en, broadcasting live from rooms in the old mill. Visitors to the web site were invited to watch the camera and report any unusual sightings. This Ghostwatch had originally been intended as a one-week investigation into the mysterious sounds and encounters in the building, with the hope that Helena would be seen on camera. Many thousands of visitors responded with accounts of truly incredible events: describing a young woman who is certainly not an employee today in the building, commenting on patterns and light on a wall or floor, or noticing objects moving in the warehouse. It would be easy to discount these reports as the overactive imaginations of people who want to believe in ghosts, but too many visitors have been in touch with similar accounts.

The following reports were received from visitors who watched the live camera on the internet:

"I was casually looking at your webcam on your ghost in the linen mill site. I saw something that scared me. It was in the corridor. I saw a woman's face and an outline of her body. She seemed to be floating there with her head turned to the side".

"I have been watching this room for the past hour and a half, and finally had to bring in my staff to see if they saw what I saw. A small figure of child or young woman crouched on the floor to the left of the photo. When I approached my staff on this, I didn't tell them where to look. Maybe we are seeing markings on the floor but this kind of draws your attention to it".

"I saw the shape barely of a lady kneeling dressed in an old style clothing, like a dirty bluish-grey dress with dark hair pulled up in a bun. She was near the back of the room".

Since the Ghostwatch began, Helena seems to have become more daring and even more active. Taunting staff with her presence, reminding them she is not too faraway. With interior reconstruction and decoration due to begin in the old mill, several members of staff have been working on

Saturdays packing files, film and books out of the way for the builders. These weekend workers have been on all floors and they all have had their own encounters with Helena. They have heard a voice yell in distress and a voice humming softly, the lift travelling from the second to third floor and footsteps shuffling on the stairs. However the most unusual event in the mill has been the extreme fluctuations in temperature. Caitlín, the editor, and Ali, the accountant, were busy sorting artwork in the design studio. Ali explained: "It was quite a warm morning, we'd been very busy packing boxes and dragging these into the storeroom. We stopped to drink chocolate about 11 and then we went back into the studio about 11.30. When we went in there, we suddenly felt chilled and remarked on the dramatic change in temperature. The room was ice-cold, it felt as if a very cold wind was blowing through the room but there weren't any windows open. I thought I would need to put my coat and gloves on. We shivered for the rest of the day, the cold remained. No matter how hard we worked we did not feel warm again. It was not even a cold day outside but the room was like ice".

The storeroom is at the back of the linen mill on the second floor. There is a corridor between the storeroom and the design studio and offices. The corridor is unlit by sunlight and is always cold. Ali and Caitlín were in the storeroom; organising printing archives and shredding out of date material. They walked in and out of the storeroom all day, carrying boxes of notes and files. They were both aware of an inexplicable heat in the dark corridor. They stopped a few times and breathed in the heat; a cosy, scented warmth, that was familiar to them. Eventually Caitlín identified the heat. The warmth of a gas fire, burning candles, melted wax and sweet incense recalled the inside of an old chapel.

Ali and Caitlín will not be easily convinced that these events can be rationally explained. They believe it was Helena's anguish on the stairs they overhead and that she moved the lift to remind them that she remained in the mill. Ali and Caitlín have their own explanation for the startling chill in the studio and the warmth in the corridor; they are certain that the extreme temperatures indicated Helena's presence, that she was with them while they worked.

Bibliography

Barrington, Jonah et al., *Recollections of Jonah Barrington*, Talbot Press

Bowen, Elizabeth, *The Shelbourne*, Harrap

Byrne, Patrick, *Irish Ghost Stories*, Mercier Press

Edwards, R. Dudley, *Daniel O'Connell and his World*, Thames and Hudson

Feversham, The Countess of, *Strange Stories of the Chase*, Geoffrey Bles

Fingall, The Countess of, & Hinkson, Pamela, *Seventy Years Young*, Collins

Franciscan Fathers, *Franciscan College Annual*, Franciscan Fathers, Gormanston, Co. Meath

Guinness, Hon. Desmond & Lines, Charles, *Castletown*, Irish Georgian Society

Hall, Mr and Mrs, *Ireland*, Sphere

Hamilton, John S., *My Life and Other Times*, Donegal Democrat, Ballyshannon

Holzer, Hans, *The Lively Ghosts of Ireland*, Wolfe

Ingram, John H., *The Haunted Homes and Family Legends of Great Britain*, W. H. Allen

Irish Tourist Board, *Ireland*

Joyce, James, *A Portrait of the Artist as a Young Man*, Jonathan Cape

Kelleher, D.L., *The Glamour of Dublin*, Talbot Press

Leslie, Sir Shane, *Ghost Book*, Hollis and Carter

Leslie, Sir Shane, *The Film of Memory*, Hollis and Carter

Little, Dr George A., *Malachy Horan Remembers*, Gill

MacGregor, Major, *Real Ghost Stories*, (publisher unknown)

McManus, Seamus, *Heavy Hangs the Golden Grain*, Talbot Press

Meehan, Denis, *Window on Maynooth*, Clonmore & Reynolds

Moore, Thomas, *The Poetical Works of Thomas Moore,* Frederick Warne

O'Connell Schools, *O'Connell Schools Union Record*, O'Connell Schools, Dublin

Old Dublin Society, *Dublin Historical Record*

Reynolds, James, *Ghosts in Irish Houses*, Farrar, Straus and Giroux

Smithson, Annie M.P., *Myself and Others*, Talbot Press

Underwood, Peter, *Gazeteer of Irish and Scottish Ghosts*, Souvenir Press

Watney, Marylian & Sanders, *Horse Power*, Hamlyn